Chasing Fenn's Treasure

One Woman's Insight into Forrest Fenn and His Poem

To

Forrest Fenn,
who created the adventure of a lifetime, and who
encouraged me to write this book...

and

my parents, who always thought I'd be the one...

CONTENTS

Introduction

It was January 16, 2013, when I first heard about Forrest Fenn. I was standing in the hallway, propped up against the wall just outside the conference room where several of my co-workers were starting to gather prior to our monthly meeting. I was not particularly happy to have to arrive to work 2 hours prior to the start of my shift that afternoon but exchanged pleasantries with the guys as we waited.

I smiled as one of my favorite co-workers approached... Bob smiled back with a mischievious grin, like he had something compelling to tell me. He slid in close beside me and started telling me about this wealthy ex-art dealer named Forrest Fenn who lives in Santa Fe... who hid a treasure chest worth a purported $2 million somewhere in the mountains north of Santa Fe. I listened intently as he explained how Fenn wrote a book with a cryptic poem that if deciphered correctly would lead you to his treasure.

Bob was in mid sentence when the door opened, and we were ushered inside to begin the meeting... I took a seat beside him. When the meeting finally ended, Bob explained he had to go... had to be home by a particular time. He told me to Google "Forrest Fenn treasure" when I had time that night at work... I couldn't wait!

Here it is almost five years later. I spent countless hours researching Forrest Fenn, reading his books, studying maps and Google Earth, and taking multiple trips into the mountains of northern New Mexico, searching for Fenn's treasure chest. I have made more than one hundred trips... boots-on-the-ground, maps in hand, solutions to the clues in the poem in my head.

After many of these trips, I wrote a story about the experience, or relayed the details to Forrest Fenn in an email.

Here are some of my favorites...

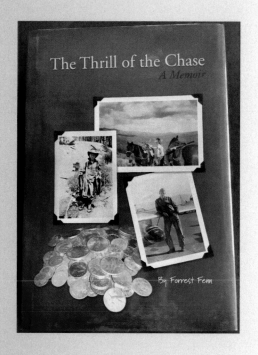

Forrest Fenn's Poem

As I have gone alone in there
And with my treasures bold,
I can keep my secret where,
And hint of riches new and old.

Begin it where warm waters halt
And take it in the canyon down,
Not far, but too far to walk.
Put in below the home of Brown.

From there it's no place for the meek,
The end is ever drawing nigh;
There'll be no paddle up your creek,
Just heavy loads and water high.

If you've been wise and found the blaze,
Look quickly down, your quest to cease,
But tarry scant with marvel gaze,
Just take the chest and go in peace.

So why is it that I must go
And leave my trove for all to seek?
The answers I already know,
I've done it tired, and now I'm weak.

So hear me all and listen good,
You're effort will be worth the cold.
If you are brave and in the wood
I give you title to the gold.

The Game ... The Rules

It's Forrest Fenn's game and there are NO rules, but there are criteria that should be followed:

1.) The treasure chest is hidden somewhere in the Rocky Mountains at least 8.25 miles north of the northern limit of Santa Fe, NM.

2.) He eliminated the states of Idaho, Utah, and Nevada and confirmed the states of New Mexico, Colorado, Wyoming, and Montana.

3.) The chest is hidden above 5000 feet but below 10200 feet.

4.) It is not hidden in, under, or near an outhouse. It is not associated with a structure.

5.) It is not under a man-made object.

6.) It is not underwater and it is not near the Rio Grande. (new clue by Fenn June, 2017.)

7.) It is not in a cave, mine, or tunnel.

8.) It is not in a graveyard.

9.) Don't search anywhere an 80-yr old man could not carry a heavy backpack.

10.) It is not in a dangerous place. You can take your kids.

11.) He made 2 trips from his car to the hiding place and it was done in one afternoon.

12.) It is in the mountains, not in the desert. (new clue by Fenn June, 2017.)

13.) It is not necessary to move large rocks or climb up or down a steep precipice.

14.) Where warm waters halt is not a dam.

15.) The clues in the poem are in consecutive order.

"WWWH is the hardest part of the poem to figure out. If a person reads the poem over and over... and is able to decipher the first few clues in the poem, they can find the treasure chest. It may not be easy, but it certainly isn't impossible."
Forrest Fenn

Clue ONE

Begin it where warm

There are many places in the Rocky Mountains where warm waters halt, and nearly all of them are north of Santa Fe. Look at the big picture; there are no short cuts.

(MW Featured Questions 8/12/2014)

What does warm mean to you? "It means being comfortable." Forrest Fenn

I will say now that WWWH is not related to any dam.

Forrest Fenn

waters halt

Chapter 1 ..... How Hard Can This Be?

It was now March 2013. Two months had gone by since Bob told me about Forrest Fenn and his hidden loot. Immediately after that day in January, I had driven to Santa Fe and bought Fenn's book with the poem. I had been studying the poem and reading The Thrill of the Chase over and over as well as studying road maps of northern New Mexico. I was pretty sure the "home of Brown" was the Red River Fish Hatchery near Questa, and the "Begin it where warm waters halt" was Pope Lake and the tailing ponds just upstream on the Red River. I mean, how hard can this be?

It was cold and overcast that day late in March when I decided to make my first honest-to-goodness boots-on-the-ground search for a TREASURE. The idea of doing this...actually going out into the mountains searching for a treasure chest worth over $1 million was... unbelievable. The idea was crazy... I was crazy... or at least my co-workers with the exception of Bob thought I was crazy. I couldn't tell anyone... I barely told my partner.

The drive up I-25 to Santa Fe was fast and uneventful. Time flew as I made my way through Espanola and up along the Rio Grande to Taos, my mind racing, thinking about what I'd do with the chest and its contents. Would I remain anonymous? Or shout it out to the world?

As I got closer to Questa and the turnoff to the hatchery the skies became a dark gray, and a fine sleet began to fall. I was determined to keep going despite the weather. I pulled into the parking lot and grabbed my raincoat before exiting the car... thank goodness I threw it in before leaving home. The wind turned blustery as I made my way to the first building of the hatchery. I walked through the buildings, amazed at all the fish and their various sizes and ages. What a neat operation, I thought... this is their home... the home of Brown (trout.)

Returning to the car I was freezing... smart enough to bring a raincoat but not smart enough to bring a winter ski hat and gloves... and a winter parka. Disappointed, I slid into the driver's seat and headed home.

Several weeks went by before the next opportunity and better weather permitted my return. This time I took a couple friends... it was easy coaxing them along to "go hiking" followed by a promise of lunch at

Guadalajara Grill in Taos. As I drove I explained the gist of the day and the search for Fenn's treasure chest. I never knew exactly what either one thought about that... I mean the treasure chest. Did they believe me, or did they think it was a big hoax and I was crazy? No matter...

We skipped the tour of the fish buildings and headed straight to the Pescado Trailhead, where we crossed the Red River and made our way up the hillside, "putting in below the home of Brown" (the fish hatchery.) As we walked I explained some lines of the poem "There'll be no paddle up your creek" meant we had to find a dry creek bed to walk up, and we needed to find "the blaze" as we went.

We were startled to find two large rocks with a splash of orange paint slightly hidden beneath the top...could this be the blaze? We frantically pushed away the pine needles and smaller rocks aside. It was too easy...had other searchers already looked here? No treasure chest... we continued up the hillside.

Once we made it to the top, we decided to take a break and take in the view. One of the fishing ponds beside the hatchery is visible on the right-hand side of the picture, the snow-covered Sangre de Cristo mountain range is on upper left, and the molybdenum mine near Red River is a visible scar near the center of mountains. We were almost 2 miles from the trailhead and car here... Forrest probably didn't go this far, so we turned around and went back to the car... and headed to Guadalajara Grill.

La Junta Trail and the Confluence of the Red and Rio Grande

I still liked the Red River for where the warm waters halt, and wondered if Fenn meant the confluence of the Red and Rio Grande, a famous fishing spot for Browns. The next stanza of the poem reads: "From there it's no place for the meek, The end is ever drawing nigh; There'll be no paddle up your creek, Just heavy loads and water high." What if Fenn meant the confluence of the rivers is "no place for the meek"? Is the Red River "there'll be no paddle up your creek"? and the Rio Grande "heavy loads and water high"?

I continued to study maps of that area determined to find a way to the confluence of the Red River and the Rio Grande. It was difficult to get to, and I only had two choices. The best path looked like driving to La Junta Point in the upper Wild Rivers Rio Grande Gorge Recreation Area and hiking down La Junta Trail to the confluence of the rivers. It was May 12th, 2013 when Emma, Molly, and I made our first journey there.

"Begin it where warm waters halt And take it in the canyon down" -- The lower stretch of the Red River is famous for its many springs, keeping it warmer than the upper stretch, making it a favorite area to fish in the winter.

"Not far, but too far to walk. Put in below the home of Brown." Red River Fish Hatchery near Questa where Brown trout are raised. The trail along the Red River below the hatchery to the confluence of the Red and Rio Grande is over 2 miles long. So we drove all the way around, parked at La Junta Point, and then only needed to hike a bit over 1 mile to the confluence of the rivers.

"From there it's no place for the meek" ... holy crap! The trail dropped 800 feet in .8 miles, some of it with no railing and a steep drop-off. Emma did not seem to be afraid of heights!

Part way down the trail we encountered a ladder... both dogs climbed down the ladder. On the return trip, Emma climbed up the ladder... I never knew Emma could climb a ladder until this hike. Molly used a boulder to hop up onto the ledge above on the return trip. Soon after we came upon 3 tiers of metal steps... after the ladder, no problem. Both dogs proved to be very agile hikers.

Eventually, we arrived at the confluence of the rivers. This was my solution to "There'll be no paddle up your creek, Just heavy loads and water high." Both rivers had roiling waters. I kept a tight grip on the dogs' leashes because we all would have been swept away had we gotten out into this.

"If you've been wise and found the blaze, Look quickly down, your quest to cease".
I noticed this rock cairn in the top of this old tree trunk. Was this the blaze? a marker of sorts? Just below it was this mound of rocks... I "looked quickly down" and peered into the holes in the rocks. I was afraid to move any for fear of what might be in there. I didn't want to hang around any longer than necessary. I "marvel gazed" for a few moments, and we left...

A short time later, Dal Neitzel who runs The Thrill of the Chase blog read my story and was kind enough to send me a private email informing me that there are no Brown trout raised at the Red River Fish Hatchery... there are rainbows and maybe a few cutthroat, but no Browns. Damn, I thought to myself, that was the perfect home of Brown. Maybe this treasure hunt is going to be more difficult than I thought...

Forrest Fenn ... The Beginning

I first met Forrest Fenn in October 2013 at his Too Far to Walk book-signing at Loretto Inn in Santa Fe. My friends and I got there early so had the pleasure of speaking with Forrest before the crowd arrived. He was jovial and happy to talk. After signing our books, he asked what my "where warm waters halt" was; in other words, where was I searching? I told of my search to the confluence of the rivers, how I was spooked by the blaze that looked like something out of the Blair Witch Project and the eerie feeling I had like we were being watched. I had read searchers' stories about mountain lion encounters, and I knew they frequented this area. He listened intently but did not interject. Then it got busy and just before our conversation ended, I mentioned I wanted to make a dozen tee-shirts for a few of my searcher friends and did I have his permission to use the poem on the back? He told me to send him an email regarding this subject in a month or two.

I did just that late in December. Then in January I received an email from Forrest to visit him at his home to discuss my business. I asked if I could bring a friend, my co-worker Bob... he replied yes. Bob and I arrived at Forrest's home mid-afternoon as scheduled. Forrest greeted us at the door and ushered us inside. The hallway was adorned with paintings by famous artists and lined with antique chests, rugs, and wooden sculptures. I noticed the long antique table in the foyer with a strange wooden figurine and two neatly stacked piles of books beside it.

Forrest stepped to the right, opened two heavy wooden doors and motioned us to follow. As I stepped down the last of the two steps, I found myself in awe. The walls of his office were filled with antique things and old Indian artifacts. The shelves on the walls were filled with old books. His desk was positioned near the fireplace, and there was a warm juniper fire burning. The book Flywater was prominently displayed beside his computer.

Forrest took us around the room, explaining much of it with stories of the past. He noticed me look up at the high ceilings and gaze at the spider webs. He explained he isn't a bad housekeeper... he keeps the

webs so the spiders eat the moths that would eat the feathers off the Indian headdress adorning the wall over the couch... it made sense. This room was intoxicating... **Forrest Fenn was intoxicating.**

Forrest sat at one end of the couch and motioned me to sit beside him while Bob pulled the overstuffed armchair closer and faced both of us. Forrest told more stories and then asked us about our searches... where did we go? what was our warm waters halt? I told him about my trip to the confluence of the Red and Rio Grande rivers because it was a prime spot to catch Brown trout... he shook his head in a negative direction. Bob talked about his searches along Clear Creek in Cimarron Canyon. Forrest asked if we ever searched around Taos... I said no. He muttered under his breath that there are a lot of hot springs in the mountains.

He talked about how he never used trails, had been lost only three times in his life, one of them being on the Vermejo Ranch when it took only 5 minutes to get turned around and lost, and how he liked to follow streams looking for arrowheads. Then just out of the blue, he exclaimed, "That's why a woman will never be president!" Bob and I looked at each other and said nothing... what the hell did that mean?

Two hours flew by... we had to leave because Bob had to go to work that evening. Forrest escorted us up the steps into the foyer and handed each of us a stack of his books. We looked at each other in amazement... what a day!

I immediately sent an email to Forrest upon arriving home, thanking him for his hospitality, sharing his stories, and giving us the books. He replied with an invitation for me to come visit again, soon. I could show him my tee-shirt designs.

A week or two passed and I returned to Fenn's home, alone. I was just as nervous the second time as the previous visit. Again, he showed me around his office... Jackie O's brandy bottle, the book he had many celebrities sign when they visited his gallery, the books with the fore-edge paintings.

We toured his vault where I saw Sitting Bulls' Peace Pipe in its case... the beauty of the twisted wood stem almost bringing tears to my eyes. Holy smokes, I couldn't believe I was seeing Fenn's personal treasures in his vault.

From there we toured his entire home... he showed me the paintings on the walls, pointing out which artist painted which piece, including the one in Peggy's bathroom where no one is allowed to tread. He took me into his "lab" where he keeps his San Lazaro artifacts and discoveries, neatly catalogued in a chest of drawers, other items in bins, neatly labeled.

We exchanged emails daily. His words were delicious, and I hungrily devoured every one... the hook was set! My visits to his home became more frequent. I took a flask of Baileys to chug the third visit to calm my nerves. He asked me why... when I told him I was nervous, he told me that was insulting to him. I thought about what he said... it was the last time I was nervous or intimidated around him. **He called me kid... was this the beginning of a beautiful friendship?**

Sometimes he'd ask me about my latest search... I'd happily oblige... the words spewing out of my mouth faster than he could understand my babbling. Once he looked at me and said "pull back your throttle, girl". I've never forgotten that and doubt that I ever will... where does he come up with some of his words and phrases?

I asked about San Lazaro... it was a totally fascinating story as I loved Mesa Verde and Chaco Canyon. He asked if I'd like to go there... he told me I could keep whatever we find. He talked about Medicine Rock and how the Indians would go there for their rituals and ceremonies. He set a date... a Tuesday because I was still working and that was my day off.

The day prior to our scheduled trip I received an email from Forrest. He couldn't go after-all because Peggy reminded him he had company coming to his house that afternoon. We would have to reschedule. I must confess this has been the biggest disappointment in the last 4 years... we never rescheduled. I never got to visit San Lazaro, and I will never get to in the future.

We continued to meet... sometimes at the Collected Works Bookstore, sometimes at Downtown Subscription. My visits to his house decreased because I felt bad about often traipsing through his and Peggy's private home, touring his bathroom and his large walk-in closet (why does any one person need so many pairs of jeans, I wondered... and why was he showing them to me?), and drooling over the Fechin, Gaspard, Sharp, and especially the Eric Sloane paintings hanging on the walls throughout his home.

He suggested we change the venue to a more intimate setting, away from the ears of the folks around us, away from the prying eyes of the curious. Our conversations had changed. They were no longer about the treasure or the poem or the chase. We talked candidly about private things. I even cautiously told him about my partner being a woman, hoping he wouldn't stop our visits out of distaste of my living arrangement. He didn't... **I loved his stories, and he loved mine.** I agreed to a change of venue... the emotional rollercoaster began!

I hid the treasure in a place that is not especially difficult to reach. (Forrest Fenn in Westword Magazine.)

Clue TWO

And take it in the
Not far, but too far to walk.

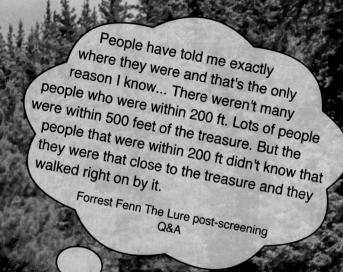

People have told me exactly where they were and that's the only reason I know... There weren't many people who were within 200 ft. Lots of people were within 500 feet of the treasure. But the people that were within 200 ft didn't know that they were that close to the treasure and they walked right on by it.

Forrest Fenn The Lure post-screening Q&A

canyon down

Stop reading the news and get out in the mountains... walk the streams.

(Forrest Fenn The Lure post screening)

Chapter 2 ..... Are These People Naked?

September 2014

My best friend of almost 40 years, who just got interested in Fenn's treasure hunt earlier this year, had been vacationing in Albuquerque for a couple months. He knew I've been an avid Fenn-fan and boots-on-the-ground treasure hunter for the past couple years, and suggested we put our heads together, figure this thing out, and go on a treasure hunt before his return home to Pennsylvania in a couple weeks... this is our story.

Even though Tom was fairly new to the search, like myself when I started, he read everything on Dal's blog. I imagine it took weeks this late in the game. We both agreed there are tremendous solutions by many tenacious searchers on Dal's blog, and we used some of those solutions and ideas with a few unusual twists to create our search area that we hoped would put us at a unique location... thus allowing us to find the treasure.

Forrest's favorite activities when he was a boy were fly-fishing, collecting arrow heads, and swimming in the warm river waters of Yellowstone National Park... making his "special places" mostly in and around YNP.

...so we pondered... what area in New Mexico compares to it?

The most likely is the Valles Caldera... a 15-mile wide volcanic caldera in the Jemez Mountains of northern New Mexico, where hot springs, streams, bogs, and volcanic domes dot the caldera floor, with some of the best fly-fishing in the state.

Forrest spent quiet days here fly-fishing back in the day when this area was privately owned by the Dunigans and may have spent time here searching for arrowheads or soaking in the various hot springs... a "special place" for those seeking solitude and serenity while enjoying the peacefulness and extraordinary beauty of this fisherman's paradise... this was our start... "As I have gone alone in there".

Unfortunately, this sprawling ranch was later sold to the government, and in the year 2000 became the Valles Caldera National Preserve. In mid-July I tried to search Alamo Bog and Canyon there, only to find out there are many restrictions and that most of the preserve is off-limits to the public... so we had to think outside-the-box. Our WWWH was the Caldera Ring Fracture inside the preserve, but just outside this ring is the preserve boundary, and just down the canyon from it, lays San Antonio Hot Springs...

San Antonio Creek flows from inside the Valles Caldera, down the canyon (And take it in the canyon down) and is accessible by driving there (Not far, but too far to walk).

Despite the 4-mile drive back a horribly rutted dirt road that only a 4-wd vehicle could tolerate, these hot springs seem to be quite popular. They are easily accessible after a short half mile hike from the parking area and a short climb up the hillside. No matter, though, as this is not the special place we think Forrest hid his treasure as it is too public and there is a trail to it. We needed to find a hot spring nearby but not on a map... maybe a smaller one about 500 ft from this place, with no human trail in close proximity... our search had begun.

There is an old cabin (built by the CCC in the 1930s) at the bottom of the hillside, about 500 ft from the trailhead that leads to the Hot Springs... could this be Fenn's home of Brown? Despite being vandalized over the years, it still stands proud and sturdy among the tall pine trees surrounding it. "Put in below the home of Brown" resonated in my head...

What if Forrest "put in" a clue "below" it, something like a "drawing". After all, the poem states: "From there it's no place for the meek, The end is ever drawing nigh;" Even though this seemed unlikely, I had to satisfy my

curiosity and peek into the dark, dank crawl space beneath the cabin. As I brushed away the spider webs and rodent feces to gain access to this little window of a spot, I held my breath and realized this was definitely "no place for the meek"...

Not surprisingly, I couldn't find anything helpful in our quest, so we moved on with our search.

We made the easy climb up the hillside to the hot springs, following the voices we could hear in the distance. I gave them a friendly glance... Holy cow, are these people naked? They were... I used a different photo for this story. We chatted briefly with the folks... oblivious of our cameras and indifferent of our story of Fenn's hidden treasure.

We moved further up the hillside and searched the base of the towering rock face above us, looking for shallow caves hidden

by the pine trees, and peering inside those that we found, only to find emptiness...

I used binoculars to scour the cliffs on both sides of this little valley, looking for the blaze to point us to the right spot... but could find none.

In my earlier searches, I thought the blaze might be a trail, but not since Forrest answered "in a word-yes', after being asked "Is the blaze one single object?" We needed to find a white streak in the cliffs, or a wall of petroglyphs pointing us to the trove...

Continuing on, we hiked through the tall grass up along San Antonio Creek to where the power lines that began at the CCC cabin took a 90 degree turn to cross the ridge, looking for a hidden hot spring up the hillside, a spot special to Forrest, one that he would always consider to be his alone. This was our "There'll be no paddle up your creek, Just heavy loads and water high."

As we moved along the creek, we knelt down and felt the water in each of the little streams that trickled down from above, until we found one with warm water...

Excited, we bushwhacked our way up the hillside, through the trees and brush to its source, only to find the warm water seeping out of the ground beneath a pile of boulders, with its opening hidden by tall ferns and reeds of grass.

... once again, I swept the spider webs from the entrance and peered in... large enough for the treasure chest but not big enough for Forrest to lie down beside it. Besides, we were looking for a pleasant hot pool of water for soaking, not a foul-smelling hole in the rocks... disappointed, we continued on.

After searching for several hours in this area, we called it a day... a bit disappointed but not discouraged.

Tom, my friend and photographer for this search... who took most of these magnificent photographs. Thank you!

Post Script

Not long after this, I met Forrest at Collected Works Book Store in Santa Fe. And once again, I enthusiastically relayed this search story to him. When I discussed the CCC cabin as being the "home of Brown", he immediately said, "don't you remember, I said it can't be associated with any structure." Hmmm... does that mean NONE of the clues can be associated with a structure? Later I talked to a local woman who used an Indian ruin as her home of Brown... she confirmed he reminded her of that same statement: "The hidden treasure is not associated with any structure" ... period! IMO (In my opinion), he is saying "NONE of the nine clues can be associated with any structure."

This goes back to one of my earliest visits at his place in 2014. He sternly told me then I had to learn to read the poem. I had to read every word. Then he asked me what is the difference between the word "the" and the word "a"? I sat there like a scared student, afraid to answer... because I didn't know the answer. He explained, "The word "a" is plural and the word "the" is singular. Oh, I thought to myself.

Upon arriving home that day, I tried to "read" the poem and get a better understanding of the lessen I'd just received. OK, I understood. The home of Brown is an actual place, or at least the location of an actual place which at one time may have had a structure residing there... just like the place called Beatty's Cabin in the Pecos Mountains just north of Santa Fe. There's no longer a structure there, but that spot is still marked on the map as "Beatty's Cabin" and all of us who hike across Hamilton Mesa in pursuit of our dreams will understand the location of Beatty's Cabin.

I made other searches as well in various areas of the Jemez Mountains, and the Rio Grande gorge... places many other treasure hunters had searched and would continue to search.... Spence Hot Springs just upstream from Battleship Rock, Black Rock Hot Springs near the John Dunn Bridge, Manby Hot Springs near Taos, Big Arsenic Springs in the gorge, the Slide Trail in the Orilla Verde Recreation area near Pilar, and back the Las Conchas Trail towards Alamo Bog in the Caldera.

Each time I relayed my stories to Forrest, he listened intently and then usually gave me some sage advice. When I explained I used Manby Hot Springs as my wwwh but then drove around to the Slide Trail to start my search, he exclaimed "then I would have said "not far, but too far to swim!"

Another time when I mentioned Alamo Bog which is steaming hot, he exclaimed "but can you get in that water?!" No, I replied, it's scalding hot". Jeeze, now I understood... If I was keeping score like in baseball, I was now about 0 for 8.

Solving the poem and finding Fenn's treasure was way more difficult than I had ever anticipated... But I was not disheartened... I just wanted it even more!

I said on The Today Show that the treasure is not associated with any structure. Forrest Fenn

Clue THREE

Put in below the

Chapter 3 .... Damn, Frank!

Once in awhile I'd write up my day's adventure and send my story to Forrest in an email. This was one of those.

Dear Forrest,

I rose from bed earlier than normal this morning, anxiously anticipating the treasures Frank (from Phoenix) and I would find on our reconnaissance trip to Rito de la Olla (Pot Creek) in the Carson National Forest some 30 miles southeast of Taos.

When I arrived at the Courtyard Marriott in Santa Fe, Frank was patiently waiting for me in the bistro, studying the Osha Mountain quadrangle topographic map he'd just bought the previous day. He apprehensively pointed out the many canyons (And take it in the canyon down), waterfalls (heavy loads and water high), and beaver dams (home of Brown) in this "target rich" (lot of possible solutions) environment. He was pleased I was thrilled with the prospect of so many places.

After perusing the map and discussing our approach, we decided the best way to get to the Bernardin Lake area (could this be the blaze...Bern = burn... hmm) where the largest density of beaver dams are located was by way of Hwy 64 across Palo Flechado Pass (If you are brave and in the wood), turning onto SR434 at Agua Fria (where cold water halts), and driving south through Angel Fire to FR76, where the bumpy dirt road eventually turns southwest high up on the ridge onto FR153 to where it dead-ends near Bernardin Lake and the beaver dams... whew!

Crawling along at 10 or 15 mph on the rutted, rocky forest roads seemed to take an eternity, and made it seem like we'd been swallowed by the depths of the wilderness... days from civilization, when in actuality we were around 9400 feet in elevation in the Sangre de Cristo Mountains about 12 miles from the asphalt road (tarry scant) we departed near Angel Fire. Somewhat comforting to me, we passed a couple empty battered pickup trucks parked along the forest road, probably waiting for the return of a hunter dragging an elk behind him. A

bit creepier was passing the old beat-up pickup truck with the two hunters dressed in camouflage, who we spoke to briefly. We asked them if they saw any elk. They did, but it was the way they looked at us that was unnerving to me (probably because I had visions of the Chainsaw Massacre movie from decades ago), when in actuality they were probably wondering what we were doing driving around in that remote wilderness on partially snow-covered roads during hunting season. Did they not believe me when I said we were looking for beaver dams near Bernardin Lake? Ever since the church kids laughed at me in the Pecos Wilderness when I told them I was looking for Fenn's treasure (they were adamant the hidden treasure is a hoax), I never admit to anyone that is what I'm doing out in the wilderness. Usually I say I'm an avid hiker, looking for a new trail with few people and a lot of solitude. Regardless, the hunters went their way, and we continued on. I must admit this was the first time in my two years of searching that I was glad I was not alone.

Frank pointing out a tree cut by a beaver.

Eventually we arrived at our destination... what appeared to be a little cul-de-sac surrounded by aspens, out in the middle of nowhere... but only to us humans.

I scurried out of the car without my backpack, eager to peer over the edge, with the anticipation of a child hurrying down the stairs to see what Santa left under the tree on Christmas morning... there were beaver dams everywhere... I was in heaven!

Unfortunately, we did not actually see any beavers this day, nor did we hike up to Bernardin Lake, nor did we find the treasure trove... but what an awesome day it was!

Here are a few of my pictures from that glorious day. 11/11/2014

28

Frank's dirty windshield made a great special effect on camera

Post Script

I first met Frank at Collected Works Bookstore in Santa Fe the middle of October, 2013. We were both there to meet Forrest and listen to him talk about his new book, Too Far to Walk. The store was milling with people. I knew no one, but took a seat in the first row below the stage where a chair and microphone had been placed for Forrest. Frank sat down beside me, and we began chatting. As I look back, I recall it was an instant friendship. You know, sometimes you meet someone and immediately like them... no particular reason that you can pinpoint. When Forrest finished speaking, we hung out together, met Forrest, had our pictures taken with him, and made plans to go on a treasure hunt together the following year. He was from the Phoenix area and made two trips a year to New Mexico to search.

Three years have passed since our first meeting at the bookstore. He and I searched at least half a dozen times, spent several days together making my movie in July 2015, attended two Fennborees, and chatted anxiously on the phone once a month or more, catching each other up on our daily activities but mostly discussing where we'd search next.

The last time I saw Frank was in Santa Fe in July where Sacha and I had met him and his wife at La Fonda for drinks and dinner. Over the course of the evening, Sacha and I made plans to attend the Santa Fe Opera and tried talking Frank into going with us. It was comical listening to Frank deliver all his excuses why he couldn't go... mostly because he hated operas. None of us knew then the horrible news that would be delivered to Frank in late September... he had stage 4 pancreatic cancer.

Frank passed away Nov. 16, 2016 surrounded by family. I miss you, Frank!

The

chest is not

in a dangerous place...

It's somewhere you

could take your kids.

Forrest Fenn

place for the meek

Dear Forrest,

I decided to spend yesterday afternoon hiking along Cave Creek in the Pecos Wilderness, and search inside "the caves" where the water "halted" by disappearing beneath the soft limestone. I did not "go with confidence" since I didn't have any good solves for most of the poem's clues; however, I'd never been to the Pecos Wilderness in the 20 years I've lived in New Mexico, and I know you and your granddaughter fly-fished somewhere on the Pecos River years ago, and it looked like a pretty place to spend a day.

Even though I'd passed the I-25 Pecos exit many times, I'd never had a reason to go there... until now. What a lovely little village it turned out to be, with a beautiful monument to welcome those who entered.

The winding 25-mile drive along the Pecos River through Terrero and Cowles was absolutely beautiful. Granted, this is not Yellowstone National Park or the Tetons or Glacier NP... my expectations were set accordingly. However, the scenery along the river on this narrow, twisting road with its occasional drop-offs and beautiful vistas was in itself a wonderful byway to explore, if nothing else. (Not a place for the meek!)

I had heard that the Cave Creek Trail was a popular hike, and that I would probably not be alone, which was the case yesterday. Just after parking, a "nice bus", with the words First Baptist Church emblazoned in large letters across the top and displaying Texas plates, squeezed in between me and another car. While I was still sitting in my truck messing with my GPS, cell phone, and backpack a bunch of kids and adults spewed out the door, and raced to the trailhead... "not a good day after all" went through my mind.

As I made my way up the trail toward the caves, I encountered pockets of the church group... first the "old guys", as they put it, who were "taking their time", then some of the kids and a couple adult counselors at a good wading spot, who were patiently waiting for the old guys to catch up and slopping in the water to pass what probably seemed like an eternity, and eventually the others who'd gone on ahead. Along the way, I also met a newly retired couple from Michigan who were bird-watching as they made their hike to the caves.

The caves were pretty neat, mostly because of the streams flowing into them and disappearing into the darkness.

Eventually the whole church group, the couple from Michigan, and I were swarming like bees around the caves, exploring inside and out, and chatting up a storm. It wasn't long until it seemed like we'd all been friends for years.

I asked the counselor "with the really nice beard", as one kid referred to him, if it was ok for me to take pictures of the kids and post them on the blog (I don't have a blog but you and Dal do)... the boys liked the idea and even included MJ from Michigan and me in one of their selfies.

We all exchanged stories as to why we were there at that particular spot... at the caves. The church group from the Houston area makes an annual outing to New Mexico each year to "get the kids away from their cell phones and video games", the newly retired couple was exploring the Southwest on their way to Santa Fe, and I, as you know... was searching for the treasure chest.

When I explained to the group that a rich man who used to own an art gallery in Santa Fe hid a treasure chest worth over a million dollars somewhere in the mountains north of Santa Fe, they all snickered but listened. I told them that when they got home, they should Google "Forrest with 2 R's Fenn with 2 N's treasure"... then they really laughed and said just that name alone proves it's a hoax. I was surprised at their initial response. I'd never heard anyone say that to me when explaining why I'm out in the mountains... hmmm. I let it go.

As we all "leap-frogged" each other hiking back to our cars, the husband from Michigan asked me if we were north of Santa Fe. I explained yes we were, even though the town of Pecos is south of Santa Fe, the drive past Cowles and the trail itself definitely placed us north of Santa Fe when we were at the caves. He immediately looked at his wife, and reluctantly stated, "honey, you were right... we are north of Santa Fe." She smiled.

As I arrived at the wading spot on Cave Creek where a group of the church kids had been splashing around earlier, there were now at least as many boys playing in the creek. Just as I approached, a kid about thirteen was doing a head-stand on a slippery-looking rock mid-creek, and about the time he extended his legs up into the air for what I thought would be a pretty good head-stand, he slipped off the rock and went head first into the creek, smashing his face on the boulder. I made sure he was ok... no blood. I asked him if it hurt, and he said YES! We all laughed. I thought of you and Skippy and Donny and June, and wondered if

Skippy (or you) had ever done anything so silly... and guessed that you had. The boys were just being boys and having such a good time... without their electronic devices. I asked if they cared if I took pictures. They didn't mind... in fact, they all took turns entertaining the camera.

Eventually the counselors and all the church kids caught up. I chatted briefly with them, telling them how refreshing it was to meet a group of kids that were so nice and polite. I seldom experience this "youth niceness and politeness" when I go to the store or out to eat. Watching this group of kids play and hanging out with them for a couple hours was a treasure in itself... totally unexpected.

I left them all at this spot and continued my journey back to the car. All of a sudden one of the boys went running past me on the trail. He looked ok and didn't say anything so I figured he/they were all ok. Several minutes later as I approached one of the most beautiful meadows along the trail, there he sat, gazing off

into the meadow, surrounded by wildflowers. I asked if I could take his picture... he said yes. I asked if I could post it... he said yes. I asked him his name... he replied Gustavo. This kid had one of the most beautiful smiles I'd ever seen... if I knew an ad or model agency, I'd give them his name. Maybe someday someone will discover him... and he was one of the really nice, polite kids. His parents should be proud.

34

I made it back to my car just as it started to sprinkle. As I drove away from the parking lot, I began contemplating what a great day it was after all... because of the "church group", not in spite of them.

My wonderful day was still not over. I stopped at the little store in Terrero to take a picture of the vintage gas pump proudly standing tall above the weeds.

Then I thought I'd go into the store to buy a soda, only to find it was closed despite the "open" sign... but once again, the treasure found here were the dozens of hummingbirds dancing about my head as I stealthily moved closer to their feeders to get a better shot with my camera.

Then, back in the car, stopping shortly again to photograph the old bridge and the little church near this same little village of Terrero, which I probably would never have seen if it hadn't been for The Thrill of Your Chase...

The final treasure of my day was gazing at the Eric Sloane sky... knowing who he is and was... and often thinking of him and you and Nicolai and JH Sharp... and realizing that saying "thanks" for introducing me to these artists and places will never seem like enough.

Still searching, and remembering the good times...

Cynthia 7/14/2014

FF Quotes about analyzing The Poem and TTOTC

"Here is what I would do. Read my book in a normal manner. Then read the poem over and over and over, slowly – thinking. Then read my book again, this time looking for subtle hints that will help solve the clues." f

OH radio interview Torg and Elliott:
Q. Does somebody need to read your book to find the treasure or do all the clues exists within the poem?
A. They don't need to read my book, but they need to read the poem. The book will help them, but they can find the treasure if they can decipher the clues that are in the poem.
"I have some advice. Read the book, then read the poem, over and over, maybe even memorize it. And then go back and read the book again looking for hints that are in the book that are going to help you with the clues that are in the poem. That's the best advice that I can give. You have to find out, to learn where the first clue is. They get progressively easier after you discover where the first clue is."

"There are nine clues in the poem, but if you read the book (TTOTC), there are a couple...there are a couple of good hints and there are a couple of aberrations that live out on the edge."
In your dictionary, what's an aberration? ~Serge Teteblanche
"I don't have a dictionary but my personal definition is "Something different." I like that word. When I was a kid there was a commonly used word. Crean, and it described the condition a car could get into when it ran into a ditch and the frame twisted a little, preventing the doors from opening. Modern autos are more sturdy so I guess that word was retired. I can't find it anywhere now.f (MW Questions with Forrest)

Read the clues in my poem over and over and study maps of the Rocky Mountains. Try to marry the two. The treasure is out there waiting for the person who can make all the lines cross in the right spot." (Business Insider 2/09/2017)

Chicago radio WGN interview, March 2013: m http://lummifilm.com/blog/WGN2013.mp3   Minute 10:45:
Q: Does the book give me any more information than I would get from the poem? A: "There are some subtle hints in the text of the book that will help you with the clues. The poem will take you to the chest but the book by itself won't."

It's hidden in a pretty good place. You've got to solve the riddle in the poem." "You can't ignore any of the nouns in that poem." 30:40 Isaac Cole Podcast 5/8/2017

Someone unfamiliar with your poem receives a message that says "meet me where warm waters halt, somewhere in the mountains north of Santa Fe." Would they be able to work out where to go? if they can't, would they need the whole poem, another stanza, or just a line or word to help them on their way? Phil Bayman
There are a few words in the poem that are not useful in finding the treasure, Phil, but it is risky to discount any of them. You over simplify the clues.There are many places in the Rocky Mountains where warm waters halt, and nearly all of them are north of Santa Fe. Look at the big picture. There are no short cuts. f. (MW 8/12/2014))

Clue FIVE

The end is ever

The spot where I hid the treasure was in my mind from the time I first started thinking about the chase. It is special to me and there was never another consideration. I was going to make it work no matter what. In my reverie I often find myself stealing away to that place and I will always consider it to be mine.

(MW Questions with Forrest 7/5/2014)

My church is in the mountains and along the river bottoms where dreams and fantasies alike go to play.

(Forrest Fenn in The Thrill of the Chase)

drawing nigh;

Chapter 5 -- Thinking Like an Architect

Dear Forrest,

I've been actively searching for your hidden treasure chest for almost 2 years, and, although I have found many treasures in my research and newly discovered places, I feel like I've hit a wall, and, therefore, need to rethink my approach to solving your poem.

You've said many times that if you can't figure out WWWH, you might as well stay home and play canasta. Well, I don't particularly like playing cards, and since I live within a few hours of the mountains north of Santa Fe, I sometimes take a reconnaissance trip to a particular area to see if any of my solutions to your poem fit the area. This is my story of such a trip.

You stated "...I didn't write the poem...it was written by an architect...each word is deliberate." So I have started thinking like an architect... which took me to Palo Flechado Pass.

Like the sign says, Palo Flechado means "tree pierced with arrows" which in your poem means "If you are brave and in the wood... it does not mean "trees" plural...it means "tree... just as you state ...in the wood", not in the woods. And what does an Indian brave do... he shoots arrows... need I say more... I think I'm headed to the right area.

Just down the canyon to the east is the Elliot Barker Trail and a few miles farther on SR434 is Camp Elliot Barker. If you look up the meaning of the word barker, Wikipedia states: A barker is a person who attempts to attract patrons to entertainment events, such as a circus or fun fair, by exhorting passing public, describing attractions of show and emphasizing variety, novelty, beauty, or some other feature believed to incite listeners to attend entertainment. This led me to the first line in the 6th stanza "So hear me all and listen good."

Two lines with solid solves...I'm feeling confident.

So now I needed to find a WWWH in this area... which took me to the Vietnam Veterans National Memorial near Angel Fire. Even though you reminded me recently that it is not associated with any structure, metaphorically speaking, warm waters could be tears... the tears of the soldiers, and their loved ones, who are honored here.

And in 1994 Lt. Victor David Westphall's father brought the earth from the ambush site in Vietnam and mixed it with soil here at this site. Maybe the WWWH, aka tears, is more about this "place" and not about the structure. It's a stretch but I won't rule it out… at least not yet.

There also just happens to be a landing strip near the Memorial at the intersection of Hwy 64 and SR434, located at Agua Fria (cold water)… maybe the warm tears stop where the cold water starts here at Agua Fria.

Could Camp Elliot Barker be the home of Brown? Not the buildings and structures but the "place" where the girl scout camp rests. It is described as "located in the Moreno Valley at the base of Palo Flechado Pass." Moreno means brown in Spanish… maybe I should put in just south of the camp and begin my search there.

Or…this Upper Rio Grande Watershed sign is on the west side of Palo Flechado Pass… is this where warm waters halt? I doubt it but I really liked the sign. And take it in the canyon down… this stretch along Hwy 64

is beautiful Taos Canyon. And off of it is the dirt road through Apache Canyon to Apache Pass…maybe I should search there. Or should I drive back FR706? The sign plainly says Primitive Road, Hazardous to Public Use… is this "it's no place for the meek"? This dirt road is also off Hwy 64 a few miles down Taos Canyon and is designated for snow-shoeing and cross-country skiing in winter… could that be "Your effort will be worth the cold"… maybe.

And the name Solo-man Spring… is that " As I have gone alone in there"? Hmmm.

So many search choices in this splendid part of the Carson National Forrest… and so little time before winter.

Cynthia

10/28/2014

Solo-man Spring -- As I Have Gone Alone in There

Dear Forrest,

Now that winter has descended upon us, this will probably be my last treasure search story of the year. I actually made this trip to Solomon Spring late last month, and I've been trying to write this story ever since. I don't know why I'm having such difficulty finding the right words. Maybe I'm subconsciously savoring these memories and don't want them to fade with the passing of time.

When I wrote to you a few weeks ago, I mentioned that I was re-thinking my method of solving your poem, and had to start thinking like an "architect"... feeling confident with a few of my solves in the Palo Flechado Pass area. I couldn't stop thinking about Soloman Spring, so one Sunday morning I left my fellow Bronco fans at home to go in search of the treasure near Soloman Spring, down the canyon from Palo Flechado Pass... down Taos Canyon.

Even though I didn't have my GPS, I felt confident I could find the spring by parking at Apache Canyon Road and walking along Rt64 until I found the little gully on the north side of the road, leading up to it.

A barbed wire fence ran the length of this property but I thought I was on Carson National Forest land and I didn't see any warning signs to keep out, so I found a small opening in the fence where I thought I could wiggle through, where I "put in"... only to catch a pant leg on a protruding barb, ripping a hole in my favorite hiking pants but not particularly caring. I smiled... I was alone and felt so free.

As I made my way up the hillside along this mostly dry little gulch, I didn't even know exactly what I was looking for. The half dozen or so hot springs I'd previously searched had been easy to identify both on a map and by the people soaking there. This spring was not even listed on some maps, and definitely not a place anyone else would venture.

The woods eventually opened up into a meadow, and I could see a small basin-like area to my left, away from the gully which by now had a trickle of clear water running down it. I thought it a bit odd that the spring may be away from the stream but I had to check it out. There was a pond-like depression that looked like a watering hole for livestock. I could see algae growing where what looked like a disturbance of water pushing up through the bottom. Is this it, I wondered... thinking how disappointing this is compared to beautiful Manby along the Rio Grande or rugged Spence snuggled in the Jemez Mts hidden by trees and giant boulders.

I perused it for a moment and decided I should try to feel the temperature of the water coming up through the bottom of this mud-pit near the green algae, wondering if the water is warm there. As I stepped onto what I thought was solid footing, I swiftly sank mid-calf into this pool of muck with visions of being swallowed alive racing through my mind. Needless to say, I somehow propelled myself out of there and back onto the bank, moving quicker than I'd ever moved in my life... or at least the last couple decades. Realizing I was safely back on solid ground, I laughed at my now slimy, stinking, muck covered boots and pants... feeling more alive than ever after the brief scare. This was not it, I told myself, so I moved back to the little stream and continued on up the hillside into the meadow.

It wasn't long until I came upon a large fenced in area with a steel livestock trough at the lower end overflowing with this mountain-fed water, which had been harnessed within the fenced area by a make-shift well-looking "thing". Ok, I thought to myself, I think I found Soloman Spring, and it seems like I'm standing on someone's private property.

I looked around in all directions and even though I was close enough to the road to hear the cars whizzing up and down Taos Canyon, I didn't see a soul. So why would I contemplate leaving yet when I just got here?

I strolled on up the hillside further into this meadow toward the grove of bare aspens, pondering the defined depression in the ground above the stream where the gully is now dry, but where water clearly stood some time ago. Could this be wwwh? Maybe it is seasonal.... hmmm.

I made my way to the lonely stump near the center of the meadow, and decided this would be a great place to sit while grabbing a snack and

sipping some water, enjoying the solitude and beauty of this particular place, wondering, Forrest, if you'd ever visited this same spot during the past several decades, maybe even sitting on this same stump... contemplating your "special place"...

As I got up ready to leave and call it a day, I looked at that fenced-in area with the well-thing in the middle, and thought, what if...? Would I be able to sleep if I leave here and don't go in there and get a closer look. I knew the answer as I meandered closer to the fence and that rickety ladder I'd noticed earlier.

As I have gone alone in there... no one is watching... coast is clear (I think). I felt silly as I lifted the lid on the well-thing and peered in. Is this considered a structure... hmmm, not sure. No matter, though, as I could see water down in the darkness. I'm positive the treasure trove is not hidden in water so I moved into the pit of stones below it, systematically moving each stone one at a time, poking beneath with my pole, feeling for anything solid.

Nothing... but then I didn't really expect to find the treasure chest here. In fact, if I'd read this on Dal's blog from another searcher, I'd probably criticize them with a terse comment about how ridiculous a hidey spot like this seems. It's a structure of sorts, could you have carried it in there, climbing on that rickety ladder, what would make this your special place?

As I jubilantly headed down the gully back to my car in my torn pants and mud-caked boots, I was still smiling, not a bit disappointed this time like after some searches. I had just spent a couple hours outside in the solitude of a beautiful meadow high up in the Sangre de Cristo mountains of glorious northern New Mexico... another day chasing this adventure of a lifetime... experiencing The Thrill of the Chase...

Until next time...

Cynthia

11/20/2014

The mountains are calling and I "must go"... John Muir

La Jara Canyon ... Guajalote Park

I'd been awaiting this day for some time now...another blessed day in January with a turquoise sky but warmer than normal temperatures. I hurried to get dress, complete a few chores, and throw my gear in the truck... no dogs this time. The 2-mile walk on soft snow through La Jara Canyon would likely be too hard on their feet. I was on my own, which is why I grabbed the rock pick from the garage at the last minute... my only weapon if I needed one.

The 135 mile drive from Rio Rancho to FR#5 off Hwy 64 (the southern half of the Enchanted Circle) seemed to take longer than I remembered. It was just me being anxious, though, as I could hardly contain my excitement to finally get to see the area back La Jara Canyon, even though the gate was closed for the winter, making it necessary to either cross-country ski, snowshoe, or just plain walk.

The area was beautiful beyond words. I couldn't take pictures fast enough, but I knew I shouldn't tarry because I got a later start than had hoped and didn't know how long it would take to walk to the end of the road... or to Guajalote Park... my destination... my "where warm waters halt".

Not too far into the hike, I spotted this depressed area with a fence circling it... protecting it from the two-legged creatures... or maybe the four-legged ones.

Regardless, this I have found out from 2-years of treasure hunting in New Mexico means it is a spring but not marked on my map. I wanted to get closer to see if there was water flowing through it now, so I waded through the deep snow that filled the top of my boots to get a closer look.

I couldn't see the water but I could hear it trickling somewhere beneath me. I hurried back to the road before I fell through.

I continued on my journey and soon saw these two markers sticking out of the snow drift. I moved off the road once more into deep snow to get a closer look. They said "no motorized traffic" and displayed symbols of what was allowed... hmmm, I wonder where that trail goes to? It is headed up the east side of La Jara Canyon... maybe to the Taos Pines Sub-division... will have to research it later.

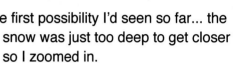

But wait, is that a possible blaze to the left of the trail? I'd been watching for rock-outcroppings or caves, indentations, any sorts of hidey spots as I trekked along. This was the first possibility I'd seen so far... the snow was just too deep to get closer so I zoomed in.

Hey, those tracks look like they were made by snow shoes. I think there are other Fennaholics searching my area. I know one thing, if you zoom in on the picture, the bronze chest could almost hide in plain sight within these gold-colored slabs of rocks (scants?)

I moved on, wishing I'd brought my snowshoes... then I could've actually made my way over there and thoroughly searched my blaze... next time.

As I walked along, I turned left, then right, sometimes even stopping and looking back, just to see the beauty from all angles, not wanting to miss any spectacular photo opportunities. And then I saw the sun's rays splintering through these aspens. This is my favorite picture from the day.

At this point I thought the scenery couldn't get any more splendid...

and then I entered the "park". I didn't think it was Guajalote but I didn't care. I might not have found Fenn's treasure chest but, to me, this was the treasure.

Looking back at upper end of park where the road bent around and ended.

But, there were cross-country ski tracks in front of me, weaving through the trees. I had to follow them, not quite sure where I was headed.

Ah, it wasn't long until I could see a fence in front of me, running perpendicular to the "trail" I was on. I got closer, and much to my delight, I actually made it to the Taos Pueblo. By now I'd walked 2+ miles in soft snow in snow boots that are made to walk from your car to the ski chalet... not hike in. I was tired... now I understood Forrest's poem "I've done it tired, and now I'm weak". Even though it took me 75 minutes to make it to this spot from the parking area, I decided to take a break, eat some snacks, and take a picture or two using my little tripod and timer mode. Unfortunately, there were no stumps to rest it on, so I set the tripod down on some packed snow, laid down behind it to frame the picture, and ran as fast as I could through the snow to get there in time... not bad, I think. I'm holding my weapon of choice, the rock pick.

Below photo: Looking left along fence line.

Looking right... this is the direction I wanted to go to the top of the hill to see if the Vietnam Veterans War Memorial is visible from down below, near Agua Fria.

I was just too tired...next time...

Jan 26, 2015

Clue SIX

There'll be no pad
Just heavy loads

When I am in the mountains or in the desert, the last place I want to be is on a trail... **There isn't a human trail in very close proximity to where I hid the treasure.**

(MW Questions with Forrest 6/28/2014)

dle up your creek, and water high.

Early retirement came unexpected that final day of March 2015. I anxiously waited outside that same conference room waiting my turn to learn my fate... leaning against the same spot on the wall I occupied in January 2013, when I remember first hearing about Fenn's hidden treasure. The door opened. I entered and nervously took a seat across the table from my boss. My heart raced as I barely heard a word... downsizing... necessary reduction in personnel... then the magic words "severance package". I listened intently to every detail as the smile on my face grew from ear to ear. Finally we were done. With a final shake of my boss's hand, I bolted out the door. My first call went to my partner. The second call went to Forrest Fenn... I was now the happiest full-time Fenn treasure hunter on the planet.

The High Road to Taos

Like many of us Fenn treasure hunters, I can't wait to get out there again and head to my new primary search area in the mountains north of Santa Fe. So upon waking this morning, I decided to drive to my primary search area high in the Sangre de Cristos to check out the snow depth there, with hopes of heading there in a week or two.

Since I had lots of time today, I decided to travel to my destination via the scenic byway called The High Road to Taos, one of the most spectacular routes in the Southwest, winding through the rolling hills of the high desert mesa, through tiny hamlets and villages, and eventually through part of the Carson National Forest, before dropping back down to Taos.

I have driven The High Road to Taos many times, and never tire of its beauty. My eyes can't seem to absorb the splendor quick enough to fill my brain, just as pictures cannot capture the exquisite uniqueness and enchantment of this high desert landscape. As I was driving along in awe and stopping here and there to take pictures, the village of Cundiyo popped into my head... where Eric Sloane had drawn a picture of the church there, and Forrest published that drawing in Seventeen Dollars a Square Inch. I had never been there but after seeing Eric's drawing, it was on my list of places to see, someday... and today was that day.

As I entered the little village, the road abruptly went from two lanes to one lane, with the buildings built right along the twisting, narrow street... making it seem like a quaint little European hamlet, but not... some of the places probably hadn't seen new paint for decades, and it was obvious there wasn't a designated crew for litter pick- up... but, nevertheless, it was worth the visit.

I had parked in a small area across from the church and decided to walk the dogs through this quaint little town to take more photographs, only there was a large dog, unleashed, standing in the middle of the street, intently watching us as we got closer. I stopped to contemplate the situation... my dogs are friendly, but... About this time a car began to drive by so I sort of waved. The car stopped, a lady rolled down her window, so I asked her where the road went if I kept going north. She asked where I wanted to go. I explained anywhere, I didn't care. I had stopped to photograph the church, and oh what a lovely little village this was. She and her adult daughter seemed more than happy to chat. They explained where the road went, if I went left or right at the t-intersection, and

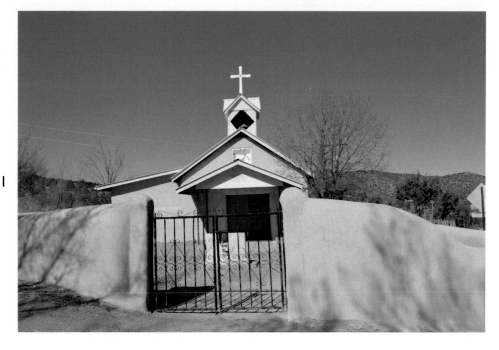

that there was another church in Rio Chiquito just before getting back up on the High Road to Taos. I also asked if they knew the dog that was still staring at us from the middle of the street... they didn't know, and the lady said that even if we got past that dog, there were more unleashed ones to venture past if we went farther. I made the decision right then to forget the walking and do more driving for

pictures... so back in the truck we went.

Not far from there, we encountered these two places, across the street from each other, both unique in their own way.

Traveling on, we soon came to the village of Cordova. Eric also made a drawing of a church in Cordova so we took the main road through town, only I never saw a church, but we did find a cemetery... one of the most colorful ones I'd ever seen.

Somewhere between this cemetery and Truchas, I noticed a van at an odd angle off the side of the road. A young man leaning against the side eating an apple looked at me and sort of waved. I stopped, rolled my window down, and looked curiously at him. He wondered if I could pull him out of the dirt embankment his front wheels were immersed in. I thought for a moment and said I'd pull off the road to see. Happily, I found the heavy duty tow chain I carry beneath the back seat, assuming that some day I would be the truck needing pulled out of a snow drift or mud-hole. Out of all the times and miles I carried this, I never used it, so was delighted to finally be able to rescue some poor soul from his misfortune... and misfortune it was. Seems it was unlucky John Gray's first day of work as a delivery man, and he wasn't familiar with the area. He thought he could make a u-turn there in that muddy turnout and soft dirt bank. It didn't take long to attach the chain to his back bumper and my tow-hooks. He asked me to go slow, so as to not pull the bumper off his employer's van. It made me nervous. He watched as the chain grew taut, hollered when it was good, jumped in the van and put it in neutral, and gave the go-ahead to proceed. I was so pleased when his 4 wheels were on solid ground, and I smiled since the van's bumper was still attached. He was grateful... I felt like a hero.

Continuing our journey, we soon started the uphill climb to Truchas... made famous in Robert Redford's movie, The Milagro Beanfield Wars. I love this picturesque-in-its-own-way little village.

We traveled through many other small villages as we made our way to the Carson National Forest stretch of the High Road to Taos. The higher in elevation we went, the more snow we encountered. These kids looked like they were having a blast.

Finally we got to Taos. As I was waiting for the light to change, I decided to take a picture through the windshield of Pueblo Peak aka Taos Mountain.

At this same intersection, I turned east to head over to my route. I noticed an old, skinny, hippie-looking guy standing on the corner, hitchhiking in the direction I was headed. I didn't give it much thought since I NEVER pick up hitchhikers. I pulled into the Visitor's Center parking lot to send a text. When I pulled back out onto the street five or so minutes later, he was still standing there holding his plastic grocery bag containing a couple cans of Fosters, smoking his cigarette down to the filter. I rolled my window down and asked him where he was headed. He said one and a half miles up the canyon. I said I was going that way if he'd like a ride. I asked if he minded sitting beside a big dog. He did not mind. I asked him if he minded putting out his cigarette (heck, it had to be burning his fingers and lips by now)... he said no, he didn't mind and tossed the butt on the ground. I pulled Molly out of the passenger seat beside me so the fellow could get in. Despite missing most of his teeth, he was a chatty fellow and wondered where I was from... we chatted. He offered that he is a poet but never published, and wondered if I'd like him to recite a poem to me while I drove. I said that would be nice. He had a pleasant voice and nice delivery. It was a poem about the old days, and buffalo that roamed, and Indian spirits, automobiles, and new highways. I wish I would've asked him if I could record it on my phone... it was delightful. I asked him if he had heard of Forrest Fenn, a famous poet and author who lives in Santa Fe who has published several books, mostly about the Taos Society of Artists from a century ago... sorry, Forrest, he did not know you. We reached his destination and I dropped him off. He was the icing-on-the-cake, so to speak, of my pleasant day. His name was John Mason, just in case he ever gets published... and I will always look for him on that corner in case he needs a ride home.

On up the canyon we ventured... my dogs Molly and Emma and me. I was still hopeful of a search next week in this area. The snow was minimal, until I got here..............

I think it might be May until this snow has melted and we can find the blaze. Until next time...
Cynthia (and Emma and Molly) March 2015

Back on page 42 I told the story about searching in La Jara Canyon in the snow. Here it is the end of April... my search continued.

FF Treasure Hunt La Jara Canyon Search Number Four

Dear Forrest,

Now that spring is here and the snow is rapidly diminishing at the higher elevations in the Sangre de Cristo mountains north of Santa Fe, this year's race to find your treasure chest has begun. I feel like I'm so close, but oh, still so far away from the trove. So last Thursday, off I went once again to one of my favorite search spots in Taos Canyon, FR#5 La Jara Canyon Rd.

I drove the FJ Cruiser this time... no dogs with me, and I thought maybe my vanity plate TTOTC would bring me the luck I needed to find the blaze.

The gate is STILL closed... when will the forest service open the gates? These closures are making my searches much more grueling than they ought to be, but they won't stop me. I just need to carry more energy bars! (I've seen other vehicles parked here over the previous weeks. I bet other searchers are looking in "my" canyon.)

Well, I guess it didn't much matter that the gate wasn't open, as this fallen tree was just beyond the gate. And unlike Diggin Gypsy, I don't carry a chainsaw with me.

I took several side-trips up the various "draws" to find a "special place" or a blaze. I didn't expect to find any such thing but had to look so It can be ruled out the next time I hike back this canyon.

It wasn't long until I reached my favorite "Blaze" in this canyon… the only rock-outcropping (which can be seen below, in the background.) But this time I concentrated on "Look quickly down", so I searched the stream in this area where the rocks formed a cascade and looked like the color of the bronze chest… and you did say you know "it's wet".

Whoa, just a few yards upstream from it was this 10 x 10 looking "rock", so I felt beneath it to assess its thickness… not 5 inches thick, but my rock pick hit something solid beneath it. I anxiously moved this top stone off, almost holding my breath to discover the secret hidden beneath it… alas, only another rock. I moved on up the canyon, eliminating this particular spot from my future searches here.

From there I picked up the pace as I knew I still had another mile to get to the "heavy loads and water high" and my principle search area. For some reason, this time my backpack felt really heavy and hung uncomfortably off my shoulders…maybe it was the pair of binoculars I threw in at the last minute. Regardless, I kept thinking how I need to get in better shape…get back to more disciplined work-outs. How will I carry out the 42 pound treasure chest if I can't even wear my backpack without thinking how heavy it is? Hmmm…getting old really sucks. I can remember 30 years ago when I could put 40 lb bags of dog food on each shoulder and stand up and walk… not anymore.

As I approached my turn to cross the levee at my water high, I found this set of antlers, pointing me in the right direction… eastward, up the hill to the ridge, where, if I stood exactly in the right spot, I could see the Vietnam War Memorial and the Angel Fire Ski runs both from the same spot.

The GPS coordinates where my backpack is lying are 36.442009 and -105.336279, at 9242 ft in elevation. I did not purposely arrive at this exact spot… the antlers took me there. OK, just kidding about the antlers, but the location I arrived at was random to some point. There was no trail leading to the top of the ridge. I just sort of picked my way through the trees to the top of the ridge.

An adrenalin rush jolted through me to what I thought could be an on-coming heart attack when I looked out and could see the Vietnam War Memorial straight ahead through the trees, and over to the right of it, the white, snowy ski runs of Angel Fire Ski resort.

60

This "blaze" of mine has been in my head for a long time, and on my fourth search of this canyon, I finally found it. If I stepped sideways either left or right one foot, I could not see both places at the same time, so I felt like this exact spot was the real "blaze". I think the Angel Fire Ski Runs could be the blaze, but you can see them from many different locations so I had to be "wise" to find the right spot to view them. I always felt like your career as a fighter pilot in Vietnam defined you, or at least was one of the most contributing factors to defining you, so I think the Vietnam War Memorial could have something to do with your "special place". I was definitely alone at that spot on top the ridge, surrounded by the much appreciated solitude… and I could see trees, I could see mountains, and I could see animals!

I felt like some of your answers and comments on Jenny's site revealed what your special place could be like; ie, Contemplating Sabratha where you "sat against an ancient wall and looked out… so many invisible lives still are there." There was a featured question regarding "slicks", a term used to describe the Huey helicopters, one of which is on display at the War Memorial. In Scrapbook Seventy posted May 2014, you wrote a poem saying "I'll set my spinnaker and jib"…both are sails, hinting at the Peace Chapel at the War Memorial which was designed to resemble a sail.

I looked around me where I stood, smelling the wonderful smell of pine needles. The fence was the boundary between the Carson National Forest and the private Taos Pines Subdivision, which displayed numerous No Trespassing signs… but why was this section of barbed wire fence in such disarray? Should I sneak across it to "look quickly down, my quest to cease"? Is this why you wrote "But tarry scant with marvel gaze"… is the chest really hidden on private property? But what if you own this particular lot? I stood there momentarily, contemplating my next step.

The subdivision area was much cleaner and "prettier"… and there were several cut log piles within a few feet of the fence opening. I quickly moved to each pile, hastily moving the logs to see beneath. I knew it was a long shot since these wood piles won't last a hundred years, but there could have been rocks beneath the logs, hiding the treasure… no rocks, no chest.

I moved back to the safe side of the boundary and meticulously looked around. There was a fire ring made of stones with the remains of an old charred log and burned remnants beneath. Did you make this 5 years ago when you hid the chest…is this the final "blaze" at the main "blaze"?

Excited, I used my rock pick to dig through the wet charred remnants. (See the antlers in this photo? Nice rack, huh?)

I took this picture to show my rock pick…I carry it in my waistband to use as a weapon if needed and as a digging tool when looking for the chest. I also had my trekking poles this time, which could take out an eye if the animal or person was so slow or old to give me time to aim…

I continued walking along the fence boundary on the safe side but never found a better blaze. Disappointed but not defeated, I made my way down the hillside and on down the canyon back to my car. I was really tired this time…this search was mentally tiring as well as physically. I think the adrenalin rushes I experienced a couple times contributed to it, but that is what this chase is all about…I spent another day in one of the most beautiful areas in northern New Mexico, experiencing The Thrill of the Chase.

Again, I thank you…
Cynthia 4/30/2015

PS…next search will be later this week …same canyon but going to follow the Rio Fernando de Taos up the west-side of the canyon to the Taos Pueblo. A long time ago, you stated "For hours at a time I've hiked through a forest looking for arrowheads…talismanic to me, and I love the privacy and stillness." This area should have been ripe for finding arrowheads, lots of Apache names… Apache Springs, Apache Canyon, Apache Pass…

Post Script after Taos Canyon Search for the Blaze

Twenty-four hours after our search of Taos Canyon, the older of my two dogs Emma took ill. She quietly lay at the bottom of the bed, looking at me with her big brown eyes, alert but not feeling her normal frisky self. I figured it was something she ate while hiking in Taos Canyon the day before. It is an area leased to ranchers who graze their cattle there, so I assumed Emma had eaten cow manure... extremely distasteful to me but nothing new to her or Molly. Another day went by and Emma did not eat and became more listless. We took her to the vet where they ran multiple tests and hooked up IVs to give her fluids and antibiotics. The test results came back. The good news was it wasn't pancreatitis, which she was prone to get, but her kidney function was below par. Another over-night stay at the vet's with IVs and tubes inserted was planned, and home we went without her, hoping she'd be better the next day.

It was barely light when the phone rang early the next morning. Emma had taken a turn for the worse, and they had to use emergency procedures to keep her alive during the night. Her glucose count was so low she went into seizures, but they reacted immediately and brought her back. We found out later our vet had spent the night with her, keeping her alive so we could see her one more time.

As we approached the large kennel Emma lay in, I could see her stretched out with tubes everywhere... her eyes were closed... she looked comfortable... maybe she was in a coma, I didn't know. I knelt down and stroked her side and said her name. She opened her eyes and looked me in my eyes... focused, and wagged her tale, just a bit, but enough. I knew she knew I was there by her side. Her eyes went closed... the vet explained what had occurred during the night, and said that she had acute kidney failure and her organs were

shutting down... it was just a matter of time. The tears ran down my face and hers as we discussed euthanizing Emma... it would be quick... we could stay there with her while the procedure was performed. We agreed.

A few days later the phone rang and again it was the vet. Emma's ashes had been delivered to them and we could pick them up at our earliest convenience. It was a beautiful morning with the clear blue skies I was accustomed to in early May. It was the typical kind of morning I loved awakening to... when I'd grab my backpack and a quick bite to eat, and then load Emma and Molly into the truck to head to the mountains north of Santa Fe. Only today it wouldn't be that kind of day.

We brought Emma home and discussed "the ceremony". We agreed that today should be the day we scattered all of Emma's previous sisters' ashes in the same area as Emma... under the giant Desert Willow tree where Emma's older sister Ripley had been buried 7 years prior. At that time, it was just a barren area of sand in the backyard. I had wanted to plant a desert willow in that spot for several years and had just gotten one at a garden store. Before the little tree got transplanted into the earth in the backyard, a bad windstorm had moved through and ripped off most of its leaves. I didn't care. I had transplanted it regardless, and lovingly watered it everyday. It looked like it would make it, despite being small. Then Ripley suddenly died when she was just 5 years old. I dug a big hole deep down into the earth beneath that little desert willow, wrapped her in her favorite blanket, and placed her in the ground.

Here it was 7 years later, and that tree had grown into a big, beautiful desert willow full of flowers. We brought the urns with the ashes of our four-legged children from the last couple decades outside. Ariel the Golden Retriever would be scattered beneath the tree on the northern side, Miss Piggy a long-haired lovable mutt from 25 years ago would settle on the eastern side, Gabby a Weimie who had died about 10 years ago would reside to the south, and Emma would take up residence on the western side, the side closet to the back porch, within eyesight of me when I sat there and gazed at the mountain in the distance.

Last autumn, Forrest wrote, "I have no desire to be buried in a box. It's too dark and cold for me, and too lasting. I would rather go into the silent mountains on a warm sunny day, sit under a tree where the air is fresh and the smell of nature is around, and let my body slowly decay into the soil."

Emma was just one week shy of her 11th birthday that warm, sunny day... the air was fresh and the smell of nature was around.

Treasure Search Bull Spring Part One

Dear Forrest,

After a restless night due to the excitement of an upcoming new search area, I arose early this morning to find partly sunny skies, beckoning me to head to Bull Spring Canyon. Unlike last week's fiasco where I ended up on top Palo Flechado Pass due to poor preparation and planning, this time I had studied my topo maps and Google Earth to where I knew exactly where I was going.

"Begin it where warm waters halt and take it in the canyon down." My new wwwh is Bull Spring, situated at 9300 ft in elevation in the Carson National Forest, off the beaten path so-to-speak, a plus when trying to find your "special place." Clue 2: "not far, but too far to walk" means there is a road you could take when you take it in the canyon down, which is Hwy 64. Clue 3: "put in below the home of Brown." Maybe the home of Brown is Bull Spring Meadow, where Bull Spring resides in its tiny fenced-in corner, and you have to put-in or park below Bull Spring Meadow, which means parking at the bottom of Bull Spring Canyon.

Molly and I "put-in" here, the same parking area we used to hike back OK Canyon. But this time we listened good... and heard you saying "GO backwards"... So we did!

After lifting the barbed wire latch, the gate fell to the side and Molly and I wiggled through the narrow opening. I was afraid the meadow might have standing water after the

last two days of storms, but to my pleasant surprise, it didn't.

We made our way through the tall grass and found a place to step across the Rio Fernando de Taos... no wading or jumping required.

After crossing the stream, we continued straight across the grassy area to the tree-line, where we made an immediate right onto a game trail, and around the corner to Bull Spring Canyon. Here we began our ascent up the canyon to find Bull Spring and its meadow.

It was a pretty little canyon, not as steep as I expected, filled with aspens and pine trees, with a seasonal stream flowing along the edge... "there'll be no paddle up your creek."

There is a bicycle trail of sorts running along the canyon floor, but it was difficult to discern it from the various game trails along the way, so I built cairns every now and then, just to make sure I could return the same route.

In less than an hour we entered the bottom of Bull Spring meadow, and oh, how beautiful it was despite the partially cloudy sky. With the recent rains, it was green and the air crisp.

We made a left upon entering the meadow, continuing our journey to our wwwh... Bull

Spring. Like the other springs I've searched in pastures, this, too, was surrounded by a barbed wire fence. We looked around and then continued uphill into Bull Spring Meadow.

Bull Spring Meadow is huge. I expected to see a herd of elk, or maybe a few

mule deer milling around... nothing.

I felt like I was in the middle of the wilderness... wrapped in solitude, the noise of the traffic left behind as we climbed up Bull Spring Canyon.

68

There were several "ponds" on top the ridge... my "water high."

The fence is the "grant boundary" between Taos County and Colfax County. Many times you mentioned the word "president"... maybe it is in reference to President Grant... a hint for a "grant" boundary.

And this gate in the fence is the beginning of the Elliot Barker Bicycle Trail #1, so you "could ride your bicycle here and throw it in the water high when you are through with it."

This is the sign before crossing over into Colfax County.

We went through the fence opening and continued walking across the meadow for a few more pictures and to see the other water high on the Colfax side. We turned around here and headed home.

I was in no hurry to get back, so I unleashed Molly and let her run free, to smell the good smells and lead the way down the canyon. Slowly meandering along in deep thought about your poem and possible solutions, we ended up at this grove of aspens.

Whoa, look at the aspen growing out of the ground at a 45º angle. It is the shape of a "Y" (wise), and there is a piece of barbed wire hanging from its upper limb down to the ground. Did you wrap that around this tree many years ago? Does this mark your blaze? Is this the hint from SB126 where you displayed Mildew and her bob-wire hat band? I mean, who would use bob-wire for a hat band? It has to be a hint!

I looked quickly down "for my quest to cease"... and found bones.

And an old rusty lid from a 5-gallon bucket... was the rust on your britches from sliding down the fire escape a hint? I used my rock pick to move the lid... nothing but damp dirt beneath it.

We called it a day... no treasure chest found... this time.

I barely put a dent in this search area. I will go back in a few days to search again. I will spend my summer searching this meadow and Bull Spring Canyon.

And like many others who have searched and gone home empty handed, I will continue to analyze the poem, and TTOTC, and your scrapbooks, and think, and read, and dream...

Cynthia
5/17/2015

The Hunt... Searching for Fenn's Treasure

By the summer of 2015 I had made over a dozen searches in the Taos Canyon area including the side canyons of La Jara, Ok, and Bull Spring. I felt I had searched the area thoroughly and had to move on. But, I wanted to share my ideas and the beauty of this area. Then the idea of making a movie popped into my head. It would be a docu-drama, like the Blair Witch Project. I needed a couple other groups of volunteers to search their areas and allow me to go with them and film their adventures for my movie.

Forrest had just received an email from two ladies from Phoenix who planned a trip to the SF area in July with their 10-yr old son Thomas. He suggested we get in touch with each other.

They were excited to let me tag along with them while my cinematographer Michelle followed. They searched the rusty cars and cemetery in Elizabethtown, and the following day along

Clear Creek Trail in Cimarron Canyon.

Since then we've become good friends and spend Thanksgiving and a summer and fall vacation together.

People: Tracie, Thomas, Molly
Golden Retrievers: Durango, Greta

72

I already mentioned Frank Abel, an occasional fellow search partner. He was also planning a search in the northern New Mexico area in late July and was thrilled to lead us on a search.

My part of the movie was last. Michelle, Molly, and I spent many days that summer in the various side canyons near Taos.

I sent my movie to Sundance that fall, trying to get it accepted into the Sundance Film Festival in January of 2016. It was rejected which was no surprise, but I sure had a great time making it!

Clue SEVEN

If you've been wise

What is
a BLAZE?
**"Anything that
stands out."**
Forrest Fenn

and found the blaze

Chapter 7 ..... The Good, the Bad, and the Ugly!

Dear Forrest,

It's been awhile since I sent you a search story. Despite our wonderful face-to-face chit-chats over the past several weeks which I thoroughly enjoyed, I'd been in a funk when it came to going out on a treasure chest hunt. As other avid searchers have mentioned on the blogs, it's quite difficult giving up one's primary search area and finding a new one, but I knew that's what I had to do.

As you know I spent much of the last 12 months in Taos Canyon... exploring Soloman Spring, trudging through knee deep snow back OK Canyon, snowshoeing up the ridge on the east side of La Jara Canyon to the CNF boundary to see the Vietnam War Memorial through the trees in the distance, hiking up the trail-less Bull Spring Canyon to witness the panoramic view on top the high alpine meadow, and ultimately making a movie of these searches.

Then, Charmay invited us to your book signing party at La Fonda. What an event it was! I posted a comment on Dal's blog acknowledging the joy of meeting Dal and many other searchers so I will not repeat that here. But what I do want to mention to you that I did not say prior was the brief conversation I had with Charmay and the turning point in my mental state to start over with a new search place. I had never met Charmay prior but made it a point to introduce myself and thank her for inviting us searchers to the party. I wanted to be able to engage her in conversation so asked her about her role in San Lazaro. To my dismay, her reply to me was something like this: "In 1977, Forrest told me he had a place he wanted me to see." (She said the name of a place and it was not San Lazaro.) She continued and said excitedly quoting you "It was here where he told me he wanted to die." Well, trust me, when I heard those last few words, I about died... of a heart attack. I never expected to hear her say this... my memory is bad, but I tried to remember her exact words... I doubt that I remembered them precisely, but I know it's close.

Which is what brings me to this story... Tsawari, the Tewa name for "white wide gap" named for the broad stratum or belt of soft whitish rock that crosses the Canada de Santa Cruz. On the south mesa lies the ruin of an old village of the Tano Indians, built by them after they left their ancient home in the Galisteo region (San Lazaro area), adjoining what now is the little hamlet of La Puebla. You've mentioned some of your special places as those involving finding old Indian artifacts, or pottery sherds. I felt it was time to take a recon trip to La Puebla and the Santa Cruz Lake area, to find out first hand if this is a feasible search area... and to rack my brain for solves to the poem's clues.

I'd passed the turn-off from Hwy 84/285 onto CR88 oodles of times on my way to Taos, often noticing the sign pointing towards La Puebla but never thinking much about it. Today was different. I was delighted my route led me through a tiny village I'd never seen before, avoiding the dreaded slow-poking traffic of Espanola. The road through La Puebla was lined with lush foliage and large cottonwoods ablaze in their autumn splendor. The local folks gave a friendly wave as they drove past me, curiously staring as I teetered on top the guard rail with camera in hand.

Here the road crosses the Santa Cruz River...

The route left La Puebla and continued east on Rt76 to Chimayo. I decided to turn south here and wind through the hills toward the southern end of The High Road to Taos, and then take the road into Cundiyo.

The next picture is looking back at Chimayo, near the famous Santuario...

The picture on the left was taken near the spot where Jesse Chehak placed his tripod to photograph the badlands for the July issue of California Sunday Magazine article on Forrest. (I know because I had the privilege of driving him to the photo shoot locations.)

There were quite a few fishermen and women along the shore of Santa Cruz Lake. I wondered if you'd ever fished here. I paid my day-use fee, properly placed the permit on the wind shield, and grabbed my pack and Molly to set off to hike around the lake... it was a glorious day!

I stopped and talked to the woman in the picture below. I asked if I could take her picture... yes, she replied. I asked her name... Shelbie. She offered that she was just learning to fly-fish. I found that fascinating since I didn't know folks fly-fished in a lake (but that thrilled me since I thought that made it more likely you would have fished there years ago.) I told her I was treasure hunting. She wondered if it was for Forrest Fenn's treasure. I just about did cart wheels along the shore. This was the first person in my almost 3 years of searching who knew your name and that you had hid a treasure chest. (She does not

search, or at least I don't think she did, until now!) I asked her what kind of fish were in the lake. She wasn't sure and suggested I talk to one of the instructors. A few more steps along the shoreline and I met Phil, a retirement-age fellow who was teaching fly-fishing for the Santa Fe Community College. We chatted for awhile. I asked him about Browns but he said this lake was mostly Rainbows... hmmm. Maybe your rainbow is trout. And the hoB is not Brown trout as many folks think... me not one of them. Anyway, he explained this was "still-water" fly fishing, I think. He said other trips/lessons included Cow River in the Pecos and the Rio Grande. Another class would start next spring. I said I was interested. He also knew of you. I'm thinking a better approach to solving the poem might be to hang out with people full of information, instead of relying on the Internet.

My dog Molly and I continued our leisurely stroll along the lake... passing these fellows along the way. We

chatted briefly, and they proudly showed me all their fish on the string-thing (how's that for technical fishing lingo... this is why I need to take lessons.)

I found a nice flat rock for Molly and me to eat our snacks. She spent time slopping in the edge of the water and sniffing inside the exposed tree roots above the receded water line. This would have been a good place to hide the chest. The roots looked liked mighty tentacles, longing to

grasp "something", like a 10 x 10 bronze box.

Unlike most search trips in the past when I had a specific agenda and was in a hurry, today I spent time just sitting on the lunch rock, enjoying the solitude of our private spot, watching a few kayakers in the distance paddle around the edge and three guys in an old wooden fishing boat lazily drifting around. I'm not even sure they were actively fishing but they looked like they were enjoying their

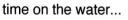

time on the water...

Lastly, these two pictures (taken from the over-look) show where the lake goes back the narrow canyon, where the Santa Cruz River enters.

There is a trail that descends from the lookout to the lake's edge. I think I need to continue my exploration of this canyon and spend time researching and analyzing and thinking about the poem.

The place name that Charmay said to me has nothing to do with Tsawari. In fact, when I googled it, I had a difficult time finding anything about it. And since winter is approaching and the search season is coming to a close for this year, I think I will make a lunch date with Charmay. She was charming, and I bet she has some great stories.

Until next time, Cynthia

Post Script: This was a private email of mine which I sent to Forrest. He liked the story and pictures and suggested Dal post it on the blog. What neither of us realized was the firestorm that it would create because of what Charmay supposedly told me. Some of the readers saw it as a conspiracy between Forrest, Charmay, and me that I was being told where the treasure chest was located. Some of the searchers canceled trips thinking I'd soon find the treasure. Some of the comments turned downright nasty... I mean vile! Some people even found Charmay's phone number and called her at home... demanding she tell them the same location she told me. I was dumbfounded!

Forrest contacted me and said I needed to fix this. The following day I went to his home and together we created a new document for Dal to post on the blog to calm the readers and assure them Charmay and I were not in a conspiracy, and that she does not know where the chest is hidden. Dal thought this would open the wound and stir the pot all over again, so I posted a short paragraph at the end of the story on the blog instead. The following document was what could have been posted, but wasn't.

The Charmay Incident

Folks and fellow-searchers,

Please stop calling Charmay... she does not know the location of Forrest's "special place" aka the hidey spot of ff's treasure chest.

I visited Forrest at his home in Santa Fe this afternoon to find out how I could fix this. I don't feel bad for myself, or even Forrest (after all... he started this with TTOTC so I think I can indirectly blame this fiasco on him... LOL, I'm kidding—don't you all start calling him... I take full responsibility). However, I do feel bad that enough of you lack the moral restraint (or maybe social decency) and profundity to actually interrupt an elderly lady in the privacy of her home and interrogate her.

In my somewhat flimsy defense, this is what transpired:

At the Gaspard book signing last month at La Fonda, I thought I would be a nice person and introduce myself to Charmay and thank her for inviting ALL the searchers to her party (she is his publisher). There were other literary folks in attendance but I didn't notice any searchers talking to Charmay, and I thought at least one of us should show our gratitude and say thanks... free hors d'oeuvres and wine, come on fellow-searchers and attendees... someone should have the decency to give her a sincere thank you. I felt I should try to engage her in polite conversation and knew nothing about her, except that she helped ff excavate San Lazaro. So I asked her how she came to be involved in it, and her reply was "In 1977, Forrest told me he had a place he wanted me to see. He took me to Lariat... we crawled through a barb wire fence, and he looked at me and said "This is where I want to die."" And, truthfully, when she said the place name "Lariat", I really thought she unknowingly was giving me valuable information. I honestly did just about have a heart attack. Like any of you, I immediately googled it when I got home, staying up well into the wee hours of the morning trying to figure out the exact spot where ff hid the chest.

When I relayed this brief exchange to Forrest, he said "Oh she meant Pueblo Largo. It's the only place we crawled through a fence. It is privately owned and near Lamy, which is south of Santa Fe."

Here's more of my defense of this unfortunate misunderstanding: Not many of you noticed this was a private email I sent to Forrest. I was not "dangling a carrot", so to speak, in front of any of you. This was an account of a wonderful day with what I thought were pretty fall pictures to show ff. I doubt he goes out aimlessly driving around the countryside anymore and thought he might like it. I hadn't previously told him what Charmay told me at the party, so used it as an introduction because it really did get me out of my need-to-find-a-new-search-spot funk I had been feeling for the last couple months.

Not only did ff like the story, he suggested I send it to Dal to share with other searchers. He had told me that Charmay knows nothing, regardless what she'd said to me... regardless what she thinks ff may have told her in 1977. Therefore, the story with Charmay was innocuous.

I'd like to apologize to those who think I intentionally misled them. Since I knew that Lariat meant nothing, I didn't think it would matter that this story endorsed by ff would raise such a strong negative reaction. Do you guys actually think that Forrest is going to encourage publishing any story from one particular searcher that includes correct, vital information that only that one person has... I don't think so.

Ok, I'm done with my rant.

There was a lot of cool stuff that came to fruition due to this. Before leaving, I asked ff if I could see The Bullet. He replied that for a nickel, he'd let me sit inside it. I never carry change but had a blank check with me. He didn't want a check... but, I got to sit in

The Bullet anyway... in the passenger seat while ff sat behind the wheel and showed me the various

accessories, how to start it, how to shift gears, and more. It was awesome. What Forrest doesn't know is that I would have written him a check for $1000 if he would have let me drive it around the block. So in a selfish way, I'd like to thank all you gold-fever jerks who called Charmay enough to provoke her to call Forrest and exclaim:

"Who the Hell is Cynthia and what did I supposedly tell her????"

In conclusion I want to be perfectly clear. Charmay knows nothing, there is not currently, nor was there ever, a conspiracy between ff, Charmay, and me to find the treasure chest.

Enough said... almost, wait, oh, in my opinion, don't ever stop searching for Fenn's treasure chest where ever or which ever state you believe it's at. Until someone is holding that chest and ff says it's been found, keep on searching!

Cynthia

Oct 29, 2015

FF Quotes about analyzing The Poem and TTOTC

Some searchers overrate the complexity of the search. Knowing about head pressures, foot pounds, acre feet, bible verses, Latin, cubic inches, icons, fonts, charts, graphs, formulas, curved lines, magnetic variation, codes, depth meters, riddles, drones or ciphers, will not assist anyone to the treasure location, although those things have been offered as positive solutions. Excellent research materials are TTOTC, Google Earth, and/or a good map.f Scrapbook Sixty Two... http://dalneitzel.com/2014/04/26/scrapbook-sixty-two/

"Well, you know... let me put this in perspective. So many people have decided they're going to take a picnic lunch out on Sunday and look for the treasure... or something to do over spring break. I'm looking' at a hundred years down the road... a thousand years, maybe ten thousand years down the road. It took me 15 years to write the poem. I've changed it so many times and I've said before that I didn't write that poem... it was written by an architect... each word is deliberate." (Collected Works Book-signing)

"If a person reads the poem over and over...and are able to decipher the first few clues in the poem, they can find the treasure chest. It may not be easy, but it certainly isn't impossible... I could go right straight to it." (Collected Works Book-signing)

Q. When you wrote the poem, did you start with the first clue or the ninth?
A. " I knew all along where I wanted to hide the treasure so I didn't need a map or any information to write the poem. Everything was in my head. It took me a while to get the wording exactly how I wanted it. Counting the clues and hiding the chest came later. It is not likely that anyone will find it without following the clues, at least in their mind." (MW Mysterious Writings Fourth Q & A with Forrest Fenn)

I said on the Today show that the treasure is not associated with any structure. Some people say I have a desire to mislead. That is not true. There are no notes to be found or safety deposit boxes to be searched. The clues can lead you to the treasure, and it will be there waiting when you arrive. (HOD Dal Neitzel's blog Scrapbook 35)

"Occasionally I forward parts of emails to Dal for use in his blog to add human interest for others who are in the search, but I never would if it made a difference or in any way might point someone toward or away from the treasure. Dal is also a searcher. I am determined to stay aloof of providing any additional clues that are useful. Everyone has the same information to work with. Some few have stopped within several hundred feet of the correct location, and then passed it by. I said in my book that the solution will be difficult but not impossible. If it was easy anyone could do it. Whoever finds the treasure will mostly earn it with their imagination. I have done only a few things in my life that were truly planned. Hiding the treasure chest is one of them. And at the end, the one who finds the gold will not feel lucky, but instead, will ask himself, "what took me so long?"

It is interesting to know that a great number of people are out there searching. Many are giving serious thought to the clues in my poem, but only a few are in tight focus with a word that is key. The treasure may be discovered sooner than I anticipated. (MW Six Questions more with FF)

Clue EIGHT

Look quickly down

Chapter 8 ..... La Caja Pueblo Ruins

My biggest dilemma: How can he "walk out into the desert" but say "in the mountains north of Santa Fe?" How can the spot be described as both desert and mountains? I think the following picture visually explains it.

The most important question: What makes the place where Forrest secreted his treasure chest "Special" or "Dear" or "Fond of" to him?

Fenn says you have to look at the big picture. There are no short cuts. This means you have to use the entire poem to understand his special place. Then you must use the nine clues to locate the specific area: WWWH, the canyon, the hoB, the put-in, the heavy

loads and water high, the blaze, and ultimately the treasure chest. I believe the poem describes an old pueblo ruin, even comparing it to his dig at San Lazaro. He has often referred to his favorite fishing places as "special places", and finding pottery shards when he planted flowers at his former gallery/home as "special". This area at Santa Cruz Lake combines both.

The Poem

As I have gone alone in there ...**And with my treasures bold**: This means he went to the spot (his special place) at least twice, the first time alone is when he discovered it, the final time was when he took the treasure chest there. Bold implies he was somewhat exposed or out in the open when he hid the treasure, or just that he hid it in the afternoon in broad daylight. I walked across the mesa top in the picture above multiple times without seeing a soul, and the only way I would have been noticed is by someone specifically looking from the Overlook Campground mesa edge across the Debris Basin canyon/arroyo onto the top of this mesa. There are no trails there and absolutely no reason for anyone to be up there wandering around... unless you are searching for Fenn's treasure or old Indian artifacts / pottery shards.

I can keep my secret where, And hint of riches new and old: "Riches new and old" describes an old pueblo ruin. Did Fenn find this pueblo before the archeologists? The first record of La Caja Pueblo site was in 1973, a year after Fenn moved to Santa Fe...hmmm. (Tony Dokoupil wrote in 2012 "From the sky, he (Fenn) learned to spot ruins by the pattern of cacti.") Is this where he can keep his secret? Is one of his secrets that he visited this place before the archeologists? Is the word "hint" implying his treasure chest is not on top the un-excavated pueblo but near it? Is his special place and the treasure on top the mesa across the river/inlet from La Caja Pueblo? Where he could sit in solitude and look and imagine the inhabitants from 800 years ago?

One of the hints in the book TTOTC which might help unlock a clue is Fenn wrote that he and Eric Sloane as his co-pilot used to fly just above the tree tops between Santa Fe and Taos. I drew a straight line between the SF and Taos airports, not the towns themselves. This area is dead-on the line. This also supports the supposed quote from Fenn when he said not only do you need a good map, you need the "right" map.

Begin it where warm waters halt: The Santa Cruz Watershed specifically at the confluence of the Rio Medio and Rio Frijoles. Both these rivers flow west out of the Sangre de Cristo Mountains and eventually flow through a wide valley where the waters slow down and warm from the abundant sunshine. At their confluence at the Cundiyo bridge, they hesitate as they combine into one river which now becomes Rio Santa Cruz, makes a turn in direction and begins the way down the narrow La Caja Canyon (also called Rio Santa Cruz Canyon on some maps) where the flow hastens and the water

becomes colder due to little sunlight hitting the water through this narrow canyon.

I believe another hint in TTOTC which will help unlock the clues is the word "warm", when Forrest describes the kids that touched the bronze and said it felt cold (because their hands were warm.) Fenn's description of "warm" waters is about temperature but relative to the temperature later on downstream.

And take it in the canyon down: La Caja Trail through La Caja Canyon. This trail dead-ends 1/2 mile downstream from the trailhead (at the bridge over the Santa Cruz River near Cundiyo) at a point along the north side of the canyon due to steep terrain. You can wade across the stream here and pick up the trail on the other side to continue down the canyon...or drive around and "put-in" below the Debris Basin, where you follow a trail and eventually walk through the arroyo to the river's edge.

Not far, but too far to walk.: This means there is a road CR503 to the "Put-in" spot instead of dangerously wading across the river where the trail dead-ends.

Put in below the home of Brown. I believe the home of Brown is the un-excavated La Caja Pueblo ruin which sits on top the mesa at the edge of the cliff overlooking La Caja Canyon. I have two different places to "put-in" that lead to the same location, sort of. The traditional phrase "put-in" refers to the boat ramp or put-in at Santa Cruz Lake. Years ago, there was even a place to rent boats there. Forrest's friend from Texas Laurens said (to our table of folks at the book- signing) that when he used to fish with Marvin Fenn and Forrest as kids, 'Put-in' referred to where they got into the boat to go fishing. I do not believe Forrest used a boat to get to the hiding spot when he hid the treasure, though. The Laguna Vista Trail starts near the parking lot and boat ramp and follows the shoreline to the end of the lake where the Santa Cruz River enters, where La Caja Pueblo sits un-excavated at the top of the cliff edge there, just above the inlet. OR, the other "put-in" is at the Debris Basin area, which is my first choice, and ends up below the hoB, but on the other side of the river inlet. Or you could wade across the river (put- in) where the La Caja Trail dead ends and end up at this same spot.

From there it's no place for the meek,: From the Debris Basin area there is a trail part way to the river but then you have to follow the arroyo to the river's edge (no human trail in close proximity), and you need a 4-wheel drive, high clearance vehicle to get to a place to park.

The end is ever drawing nigh;: Hike up the "draw" to the top of the mesa if the chest is hidden on top and not along the shoreline.

There'll be no paddle up your creek,: The (dry creek) arroyo coming from the debris basin.

Just heavy loads and water high.:The Santa Cruz Debris Basin whose purpose is to collect the debris (heavy loads) washing down the arroyo during heavy rains (water high), keeping it out of the river and lake.

If you've been wise and found the blaze,: Wise = Y's. Look at the big picture on a topo map. The confluence of the Rio Medio and River Frijoles make a Y with the Santa Cruz River. Further down stream towards Santa Cruz Lake, another Y is formed by the emergence of the debris basin arroyo where the Santa Cruz River then turns north, making another Y. Fenn wrote "If you've been wise and found the blaze..." which means you have already found the blaze by the time you get to the top of the mesa and the pueblo. Pictures of the blaze are later in this document.

Look quickly down, your quest to cease,: Here Fenn tells you to "look", not "dig" because it is not buried. Quickly down means close to the top of the mesa. Look near the edge. ff has stated in emails: "How will you know where the edge is if you don't go out there and look?" "The hints are in the aberrations at the edges."

But tarry scant with marvel gaze,: You can see the road (CR503) from the top of the mesa here. You marvel as you gaze at how close (scant) this spot is to the asphalt (tarry) road. (SB70, Forrest wrote "...Esmeralda, who still glides the tar-top..."

Just take the chest and go in peace.: Means exactly what it says...the last of the nine clues. (Caja means box or chest in Spanish...hmmm. Is "chest" the word that is key?)

So why is it that I must go...And leave my trove for all to seek?: Future archeologists who might excavate this site someday, find his bones, and the treasure chest.

The answers I already know,...I've done it tired, and now I'm weak.: Fenn spent 30 years excavating San Lazaro, until the ripe old age of 84, and knows the answers to why excavate.

So hear me all and listen good,...Your effort will be worth the cold.: The cold is the loneliness when you search for the treasure, (or you waded across the cold river to get here) but he knows the end result will be worth it just like when he discovered the artifacts at San Lazaro. He is telling us "listen to me... I have already done this", again implying the special place is an old Indian ruin.

If you are brave and in the wood...I give you title to the gold.: Brave implies Indians (pueblos); in the wood refers to the old saying meaning aged, old which is the old pueblo. Title to the gold may be a reference that gives land owners title to archeology, putting artifacts in the same category as oil or gold (like San Lazaro).

Fenn statements:

Fenn said "some searchers have figured out the first two clues but didn't understand the significance of where they were, and went right past the next seven."

"Some folks correctly mentioned the first two clues to me in an email and then they went right past the other seven, not knowing they had been so close." They figured wwwh is confluence of Rio Medio and Rio Frijoles, the two rivers of the Santa Cruz Watershed, that combine to make Rio Santa Cruz. They went downstream on La Caja Trail through the canyon, but it dead ends. What they didn't understand is home of Brown is the un-excavated La Caja Pueblo which sits atop the cliff above the inlet where the Santa Cruz River enters Santa Cruz lake. They didn't know they could skip wading across the river but instead drive to the debris basin area and walk down the arroyo to the river. Instead they drove around to the main entrance into the Santa Cruz Lake Recreation Area and parked where everyone else parks, thereby going "right past the other seven, not knowing they had been so close."

"Some searchers have been within 200 feet of the treasure". This statement stumped me for awhile, but I think the 200 feet distance is elevation. La Caja Trail and canyon where the Santa Cruz river flows to the lake is at 6500 feet, while the mesa above and treasure location is at 6700 feet.

Fenn said "there are a lot of places in the Rocky Mountains where warm waters halt and most of them are north of Santa Fe." I believe warm waters has to be something obscure by Fenn's definition but something common enough for many to occur, like the confluence of two separate rivers that combine to become a new river before flowing downward through a narrow canyon. Maybe Fenn considers the confluence of these rivers as "halting", momentarily, when they combine and turn direction drastically to make one river. Or the wwwh refers to the Santa Cruz "water **shed**".

SB116 Peek-a-Boo Art about the shower tiles. Is this a hint to warm waters (taking a shower) halting/draining, collecting water that's delivered down stream? Is it a hint for his bathroom (water closet to Europeans. Does water closet mean water **shed**?)

SB115 Proper Dental Care about his tooth brushes. Again hinting warm waters draining, and includes a photo of his frog jar in his bathroom (WC - water closet).

SB99.5 I have rules: about his bathroom (WC)

SB98 Closet Stories: about his walk-in clothes closet. Is this the predecessor about the word closet (**shed**?)

Fenn said **"many are giving serious thought to the clues in my poem, but only a few are in tight focus with a word that is key."** I believe the word that is key is **chest**, in Spanish **caja** (also means box).

Fenn wrote in TTOTC **"So I wrote a poem containing nine clues that if followed precisely, will lead to the end of my rainbow and the treasure."** Does "rainbow" allude to the state record rainbow trout caught in 1999 at the end of the Santa Cruz river in the inlet where it enters the lake? Which is just below (in elevation) La Caja Pueblo.

Fenn said **"People will be surprised when they find out where it is."** Because it is close to the road. And only about 25 miles north of Santa Fe.

Fenn said **"When it's found, people will say 'why didn't I think of that?' "** Could be the key word caja.

"It seems logical to me that a deep thinking treasure searcher could use logic to determine an important clue to the location of the treasure..." He uses the word "deep" which suggests "elevation". He often said you might as well ask him, how deep is a hole? IMO, this is the important clue to the location of the treasure... 200 ft above La Caja Canyon/river.

"What surprises me a little is that nobody to my uncertain knowledge has analyzed one important possibility related to the winning solve." I believe this to be the same... 200 ft above canyon.

Fenn said: **"The clues did not exist when I was a kid but most of the places the clues refer to did..."** Santa Cruz Lake was finished in 1929. Some of the trails were developed later.

"I warned the path would not be direct for those who had no certainty of the location beforehand, but sure for the one who did." The path is not direct because the La Caja Trail dead-ends before you get below the La Caja Pueblo ruin. You can either choose to wade across the stream there to pick up the trail on the other side of the river, or drive to the Debris Basin area and walk down the arroyo to the river where you come out at almost the same spot.

Boots on the Ground

I started searching this area in late September of this year. I felt confident in most of the solutions to the clues beforehand, but couldn't find a good, solid blaze prior to starting my searches. My original plan: hike all the trails in the SCLRA (Santa Cruz Lake Recreation Area, which by the way is governed by BLM), along with scouting the tops of the mesas that look across the Santa Cruz River inlet to the site where Google Earth shows La Caja Pueblo.

Below is a picture using GE of one of my more interesting "blazes"... a martini glass! Forrest once said on MW (Mysterious Writings) Six Questions More with Forrest Fenn: "It is important that I drink a martini at least once a year so I can continue to remember why I don't like them." La Caja supposedly sits above and just to the right of the rim of the glass.

Almost every square inch of the area in the picture above is fairly accessible, even for an "almost-eighty" year old physically fit man, except for the mesa top where La Caja sits (near the martini glass.) I've studied the sides of the canyon and the sides along the lake, looking for a way to hike up onto that mesa top. If Fenn hid the treasure chest on the un-excavated pueblo, I think he would have had to parachute in, or get there by helicopter and I am almost certain he did neither. This is why I think he wrote "And hint of riches new and old." His treasure chest is a hint away.

La Caja Trail...

I found the small parking area on the north side of the bridge just beyond Cundiyo where the Rio Medio and Rio Frijoles merge, change directions, and proceed through the canyon.

The air was still and crisp that morning as Molly and I departed the truck. She anxiously climbed the log steps from the parking area to the trailhead as I gathered my pack and slid the handle of my rock pick under my waist band. The undulating trail started high above the river. It was narrow but easy to follow. We made a few stops along the river's edge to

take pictures. There were small waterfalls and deep pools along the way. Occasionally yellow leaves drifted lazily to the ground, making a soft amber mat below my feet.

We reached the beginning of the end of the trail, where the stream continued it's flow through the canyon towards the lake. Here the trail led us through thick clumps of willows that slapped across my face and grabbed at my hair like tentacles, as it started to rise up the canyon wall.

Molly and I went as far as we could go. We looked all around us for a blaze.

There were various rock-outcroppings. If the sun hit just right, the rocks gleamed from the mica, glistening like diamond flecks... but none stood out. There were no petroglyphs to be seen, no owls (If you've been wise...) to contemplate.

We left after a short break and snack... but our day was not over. The next part of the agenda was drive to the Overlook Campground and walk to the edge of the mesa where I could use binoculars to look at the top of the mesa where I thought the old ruins stood. Previously, I had seen whitish "rocks" or something from the distance but couldn't tell what it was.

We paid our daily use fee at the station and parked in one of many empty campsites ... only one site was occupied. I could see a nice big 5th wheel and pickup truck with Utah plates. Hmmm, "maybe other treasure hunters" I jokingly said to Molly... but I really doubted it. It was quiet... there was no one around.

I picked the way across the sandy terrain, trying to be careful not to lead Molly into the low growing, creeping cacti that looked like patchwork on a giant quilt.

All of a sudden we came upon this... a marker for aircraft, maybe? Did Fenn fly his plane over this exact spot between Santa Fe and Taos when he and Eric used to fly just above the tree tops?

As we approached the edge of the mesa overlooking the chasm between the two flat ridges, I discovered the folks from the campsite. Their mountain bikes lay under a cedar tree and their yellow lab cautiously approached. The girl followed. I asked if the dog was friendly... yes. I asked its name... Ella (sounded familiar). We exchanged a few pleasantries... then her husband appeared holding powerful binoculars.

I asked if they were treasure hunting. No, she is a rock-hound and they were looking for a way to get down into the arroyo. (It wasn't JDiggins...I met her in person at the La Fonda book-signing a week before.) She said they'd just arrived in New Mexico three days ago. I asked if they'd heard of Forrest Fenn... an immediate "no"... I said google him and treasure. I told her I thought the treasure might be in an old pueblo across the chasm, pointing to the top of the mesa. I told her they might as well be searching for Fenn's treasure while they rock-hound around northern New Mexico. She asked again his last name... I replied Fenn. She said oh that's easy to remember because my last name is Finn. Then Molly and I departed to go look through my binoculars at "the ruins."

All of a sudden a sick feeling of deja vu overwhelmed me like a heavy veil. In my exuberance to pass along Fenn's Thrill, did I just give away his special place and the location of the treasure? to another treasure hunter? They already had powerful binoculars and were looking the same direction I was about to look (See very first picture... my dilemma). If they were there for the same thing, I knew the race had begun.

Molly and I continued to the edge of the mesa east of the Overlook Campground to get a better look at the mesa top across the chasm where the Debris Basin arroyo separated the two hills. The deja vu I had just experienced was still vivid in my mind. What the heck was I thinking. Too late now... I pulled the large binoculars from my backpack, brought them up to my eyes, and carefully focused each eyepiece.

It looked like rocks, or whitish stones... but maybe there were remnants of old pueblo ruins mixed in. Too far away to tell. I couldn't wait to return.

I barely noticed the ride home. I was in auto-pilot... my mind was racing trying to remember the exact words of the article I found online describing the La Caja Pueblo site. I didn't even check Google Earth for the location because the description was so detailed "The La Caja site is a large pueblo ruin located within the Santa Cruz Lake Recreation Area, west of Cundiyo, New Mexico. The pueblo is situated on the edge of a flat ridge top, overlooking the La Caja box canyon, between the confluence of the Rio Medio and Frijoles and Santa Cruz Lake. The site is in the high vegetated mounded category, denoting a series of room blocks, which here partially surround two plazas. Analysts of ceramics collected from the site suggest that the pueblo dates to the early fourteenth century." When I first read the details, I thought, oh my God, this is the perfect place for Fenn to die beside his treasure chest.

La Caja Pueblo Ruins Part Two

A couple tortuous weeks passed before I could return. Once again, my mind was racing as Molly and I made our way around Santa Fe and turned east on the High Road to Taos. This time we passed the turn to the Overlook Campground, continuing about half a mile or so to Mile Marker 9 where I made a left onto a dirt "road" that wound back into the hilly terrain above the Debris Basin. My nerves were on edge as I drove slowly through the ruts and loose sand. I desperately was hoping not to get stuck. I decided to drive up a

short but steep and tilted section of "road" and park in the trees where the truck was mostly out of sight. It looked like the main dirt "road" continued all the way down and along the east side of the debris basis where it stopped at the bottom of the mesa I was about to climb. I didn't know about pushing my luck further. Maybe Fenn drove there when he hid the treasure chest, but on this day and all those searches in the future, this would be our parking spot, and we'd walk from here. (See arrow in photo.)

It was what I considered an easy climb up the hillside to the mesa top. To my liking, there was no trail. We wound our way between the junipers and piñon trees and scurried across the top to the edge that overlooks La Caja Canyon, to the large, whitish rocks we witnessed weeks ago through the binoculars from the edge of the Overlook Campground. My God, once again, I thought how perfect this place seemed. It definitely could be his "special place". It was easy to get to... I looked around and could hear the river rushing through the canyon below me. I could see the lake off in the distance. I could see the Sangre de Cristo mountains to the east... and there was no one in sight.

The number of possibilities where Fenn's trove could be hidden was overwhelming that first trip. I did my best to scour each and every nook and cranny along the edge... in, under, and around all those boulders, even searching beneath the trees.

When I found this flat rock (is it the "scant", a large flat stone?) beside the boulders, I about had a heart attack. I was almost positive I'd find the chest secreted beneath it. It was heavy... I used my rock pick to dig along the edge. I slid my fingers beneath the edge and secured my grip. As I slowly titled the stone onto it's edge, I rested it against my leg so as not to accidentally drop it on my toes, and stood it up. My jaw dropped... I "marvel gazed"... there was just another rock under it... no treasure to behold.

As depressing as this story might sound, it was a glorious day. I had found a new place where I could sit and ponder in silence... and soak in the beauty of this desert environment. But I wasn't through... I was not about to give up on this area... this flat mesa top where I knew there had been inhabitants 800 years ago.

I made three more trips to search this entire mesa top. I moved my searches east along the edge but also searched the top where there was less vegetation. Maybe that's where the ruins sat. I searched for pottery shards with every step.

I perused the shallow draws between hilly areas where the rain water would run off the mesa top down into the canyon. I soon became more obsessed with finding the pueblo than I did finding Fenn's treasure.

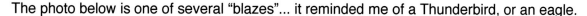

The photo below is one of several "blazes"... it reminded me of a Thunderbird, or an eagle.

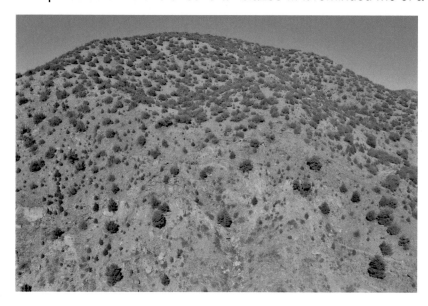

I even found a circle of rocks during one of my searches. It was the only sign of another human being's presence. I meticulously moved each rock to see what lay beneath... it was an old campfire that had been carefully covered with rocks. Maybe Fenn had been there after all. I carefully put the rocks back.

Over the course of these few weeks and multiple searches, this mesa top became my "special place". Molly and I always ate our snacks on the "pueblo floor" in the picture below. I don't believe it is really a pueblo floor but it sure looked like one the first time I discovered it.

Some days when we searched in that area, I made Molly wear her boots. Too often she'd stepped on the low creeping cacti, and it was as painful to me to remove the thorns as I'm sure it was to her. The boots worked great, and it didn't take long for her to get used to them.

By now it was the beginning of November. I hadn't even found one single pottery shard. The search season would soon be ending, and I felt empty... well, at least empty-handed.

I decided to use Goole Earth to try to find a better blaze, or something I missed that would lead me to the treasure. I tried searching GE using "La Caja pueblo" but nothing came up. Then I believe by accident I just used La Caja and GE zoomed right into the Santa Cruz Lake Recreation Area. But what the hell... it zoomed onto a spot on the other side of the canyon, closer to the inlet where the river enters the lake. I laughed out loud... for a full month I was looking at the wrong spot!

(I hope this made everyone reading this laugh. And you all can breathe a sigh of relief... the odds of me finding Fenn's treasure is pretty low it would seem!)

But wait, this was actually good news. I felt rejuvenated. I was excited all over again. I studied Google Earth. Now my solves had to be revised but I still liked this area for the same reasons. The actual pueblo site on top the correct mesa looks unaccessible. Maybe Fenn fished beneath the cliff along the inlet when he was younger. Maybe he found artifacts there when he went there to fish. I couldn't wait to return.

My new "blaze" is the cliff shaped like an "M" where the pueblo site sits above what I believe is the right-side hump. It reflects into the lake to make an abstract "W". The "M" and "W" are like the wings of two eagles... ff said to use our imagination. For Michael D if you read this, you once used Fenn's CC double eagle coins as your blaze, "If you've been wise and found the blaze, Look quickly down, your quest to cease" = 2 C's. Hmmm. My dilemma at this point: is his special place where he secreted the treasure chest along the shoreline, or on top the mesa

where he can look across the inlet and see the old pueblo ruin site on top?

My strategy was to hike along the Laguna Vista Trail which ends at the land protrusion on the left side of the picture above and try to see into the inlet along the shoreline. Even though it was November by now, it was still relatively warm. I couldn't wait to begin searching once again.

I felt rushed the first morning Molly and I made our first hike along the east shore of the lake to the inlet. The Laguna Vista trail is only 1.2 miles long and a fairly easy hike, but it seemed to take forever to get to the end. It was a nice surprise to see a fisherman drift by in his boat as he entered the inlet.

Unfortunate for me, I couldn't see around the bend in the lake inlet good enough to satisfy my curiosity at what lay below the M hump along the shoreline. Was it a place where Forrest could have stood on land and fished... and ate a pimento cheese sandwich beneath a cottonwood tree... and looked for artifacts long ago buried in the sand?

Plan B: I decided the best way to see beneath the right-side hump of the "M" blaze was from across the inlet/river. The Overlook Trail extends from the Overlook mesa west of the campground area, northward to West Canyon, then down to the lake shore, where the trail divides, one section going east along the shoreline towards the inlet... where I needed to go. By now northern NM had it's first snowfall but much of this area is in full sun, so I figured if Molly and I were careful, we should be able to make our way down the trail to the inlet.

Once again, we got to what seemed like the end of the trail. There was a rock outcropping in our way... it was snow covered and too risky to keep going. We were so close to where I wanted to be... but I wanted to be safe. The lake looked deep there, and too cold to fall into this time of year. And I'm still not sure if Molly can swim... that day was not the day to find out.

Plan C: The Debris Basin Trail begins at the basin and descends an arroyo to the Santa Cruz Canyon and river, about 200 meters downstream from where the La Caja Trail ends on the opposite shore. The trail then follows the river downstream to the lake, supposedly.

The mornings are now cold and the days are shorter. Nevertheless, my obsession with seeing the entire shoreline beneath the "M" blaze has taken control of me. I packed Molly and my gear in the truck for what I hoped was the last search of the year. As I approached Mile Marker 9, I was concerned I might get stuck in snow going to my secure hiding spot off the dirt road above the Debris Basin. I slowed, and tentatively crawled along the snow-covered dirt until I got to the section that is steep and tilted. I was already in 4-WD... I hesitated... thought what the hell, and stepped on the gas pedal. The truck made it up the tiny hill and I breathed a sigh of relief.

The trail from the basin down through the arroyo was relatively easy. There was a fence-like "weir" near the bottom, just before it met the trail along the river. At the river's edge the trail became more difficult. There were willow branches to push away and rock slides to cross as we trod downstream to the inlet.

And once again, just before the turn in the river where the "M" stood, we hit a dead end.

Stay tuned...I'm not done yet!

La Caja Pueblo Ruins Part Three

It was now December 8th, and I still hadn't been able to get to the specific location where the Santa Cruz River enters the inlet. Looking at both Google Earth and TopoQuest, the La Caja Ruins site seems to be immediately above the cliff-face at that imaginary line.

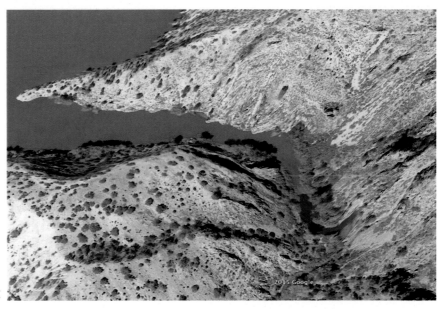

I was positive Fenn didn't hide the treasure chest on the ruins site. There was just no way up to the mesa top. So my dilemma still was: did he hide it on top the mesa edge not far from the Overlook Campground where he could sit out of view beneath a juniper tree and gaze across the river, imagining the puebloans from 800 years ago? Or did he secret it among the trees along the shoreline beneath the pueblo, where ancient artifacts may have fallen off the cliffside or washed over the edge during the past eight centuries? Did he take a boat to this particular spot to fish 40 years ago, or walk there from the Debris Basin and wade across the stream…and discover pottery shards or other ancient artifacts partially buried in the sand?

I woke to beautiful blue skies that Tuesday morning. My obsession with seeing this specific place, where the river entered the inlet, had not waned; in fact, it was worse than ever. I decided to make one last trip there. I would park at the Overlook Campground, and Molly and I would walk out across the ridge to the

point where it overlooks the inlet. I knew from there I could see both shorelines, and search for the treasure chest if he did indeed hide it on top the mesa across the river, at some obscure place out of sight of others. The red arrow in the picture shows you where I planned to go.

It was barely above freezing as we made our way to the turnoff to the Overlook Campground…no matter, though, I was psyched. I knew today was the day I was going to finally see this spot I'd been trying so desperately to reach. And then I saw it… there was a locked gate across the dirt road to the campground. My heart sank… I think I had tears in my eyes from the overwhelming disappointment. I could park there along the highway and walk the 1.5 miles back to the campground but that would add a lot of time and walking to our day, and I wasn't prepared.

Quickly, I had to come up with a Plan B. I told Molly we wouldn't give up… this day was our last chance of finding this place until springtime, and I knew my patience wouldn't hold. We drove around to the main

entrance to the Santa Cruz Lake Recreation Area and parked. I decided we could hike along the eastern shoreline again on the Laguna Vista Trail, and instead of stopping at the dead-end like last time, we would climb across the ridge-line towards the inlet, then scamper down the side to the lake edge where maybe we could see the confluence of the river and inlet.

This fallen tree was as far as we could go. I carefully stepped out onto the limb and slowly slid across the smooth bark, balancing precariously as I zoomed in with my camera. Maybe I'd see

something helpful in the picture later. From the middle of the tree limb, I squinted to see as best I could into the inlet and beyond. It looked like there was already a thin sheet of ice covering the inlet. In my mind I thought… today, this is where warm waters halt.

The hike back to the truck was quick and quiet. I was not especially pleased with another failed attempt trying to reach the imaginary line, the spot. But one positive thing did enter my mind.

Back in October, 10-yr old Thomas and I had made a 10 x 10 x 5 box, and then placed it 200 feet from the edge of the street. To my amazement, 200 feet was much farther away than I expected… and that little box was hard to see. I thought about the three trails I had hiked over the course of the last couple months there. I bet I was about 200 feet from the "spot" at the end of each trail. And another thing, the "spot" was not visible from the end of any of the three trails. Forrest could have secreted the chest there, or died there beside it, and he would not have been visible to hikers, or boaters. Few fishermen would have tried to wade across the river there, making it the perfect place… easy for him to get to but isolated. Is this where he found "solace in the solitude of the trees"?

Over the next couple weeks, I continued researching this area… looking for better "blazes" or anything that could help… using Google Earth to zoom in on the mesa top where La Caja supposedly sits.

I continued to study Scrapbook 107, one of the few I thought actually contained hints. I especially like the word "CruZ" that was formed by the edge of the envelope, the "r" in Mr, the "U" in the guy's first name, and the "Z" formed by the layout of the pen, pen cap, and $5 bill.

I reread the stories in TTOTC, and studied each and every drawing. I remembered Forrest saying "The hints are in the aberrations at the edges". I was not one to previously believe the drawings in the book were of any help… but I knew it couldn't hurt to look.

I noticed in the drawing on page 43, the woman's boot that I circled is an aberration… it is not connected to a person. Is this a hint to the picture of the inlet to the lake, which also resembles a woman's boot? Did Forrest add this to the drawing?

Then on December 17th, Dal posted the Air Force Interview. I reserved a block of time the following afternoon where I could turn off my cell phone, close the door to the library, sit back in my big comfy recliner, and listen attentively. Forrest did not disappoint… his stories were both informative and entertaining. In part three, he described with great detail ejecting from his wounded fighter jet that was about to crash into the countryside, but what stood out to me was his description of his landing spot. He called it a "karst", to us a bluff or cliff. At that moment, I pictured the drawing on page 99 of TTOTC.

Back in October, Mindy posted a story on her blog about Diggin' Gypsy. In that story Diggin' talks about her discovery of Fenn's treasure map. She surmises that Fenn is the one who drew this drawing, not the artist who drew all the other ones in the book. At the time (this was posted Oct 28th on The Fenn Hotspot), I looked at this drawing... this "treasure map". I was impressed with the ideas Diggin presented. They were cute, clever. Then I closed the book and never looked at that drawing again... until Dec 18th.

I am not going to add to my story Diggin's specific hidden gems she has shared with the world. You can go to Mindy's blog to see each one. But the one she didn't highlight was the "arrow" circled in red. What if... Forrest did draw this picture?

What if... the arrow points to his special place... both where he safely landed and where he hid the treasure? What do the ladders signify (look to right of red arrow)? Puebloans used ladders in their multi-story pueblos.

Now Diggin' turned the book/drawing upside down to understand the clues. One small scribe says "FLY TAOS". It appears the man wearing the large brimmed straw hat is wearing sunglasses (for the ArcLight?), and possibly carrying something. I studied this drawing for hours over many days. I compared it to pictures I had taken over the course of the last two and a half months.

In the drawing, it looks like a river runs between two mesa tops. Does this suggest the area where the river enters the inlet to the lake? It looks like the arrow circled in red comes out of a formation shaped like the right-hump of my "M" shaped blaze, the cliffside just below La Caja.

Do the palm fronds or the propellers in the "FLY TAOS" scribe represent this aircraft marker?

Or do the palm tree and man-in-shades dressed for a picnic represent the Overlook Campground with it's covered picnic tables… a place for local folks?

Many times throughout the past five years, Forrest has mentioned the word "IMAGINATION"…
Is "imagination" the word that is key?

In Diggin's story she says "Forrest said he melded the memories of his experience in Vietnam with his favorite spot." I do not know where she saw that written or if he said it to her. What if… he did? What if… he drew this particular drawing? What if… it is his secret "treasure map"?

To quote Shakespeare, sort of: " To be(lieve), or not to be(lieve), that is the question?"

I never had time to get to the imaginary line separating the river and inlet before the last snow fell. I do believe that ultimately someone will follow their crazy idea… their vivid imagination… their "what if…" and Fenn's treasure will be waiting for them…   Until springtime (nah, I won't wait that long)… Cynthia

La Caja Pueblo Ruin ... The Final Chapter

It was January when I last published Part Three about searching La Caja Pueblo Ruins. I was still trying to get to the "Imaginary Line" where the Santa Cruz River enters the inlet to Santa Cruz Lake. This area of shoreline, I thought, would be directly below the ruins, my home of Brown.

I made an attempt to access this spot in late February via the Debris Basin Trail. My day was cut short when I found a German Shepard caught in an animal trap just to the side of the trail. She was big and beautiful and timid. Her foot was pinched and she couldn't escape. Eventually, I found help, and she was released, unharmed. I wanted to take her home, but she bolted as soon as she was free.

In early March I decided to try a different approach. I parked at the gate to the Santa Cruz Lake Overlook Campground and walked back the road. My plan was to walk across the ridge tops to the inlet and look down at the shoreline at this imaginary line. As I ambled along the edge of the road that day, I found a $10 dollar bill lying there. Another five yards and I found a $5 dollar bill, and then a trail of $1 dollar bills... six of them in succession crossing the road to the weeds on the other side. A total of $21, I was thrilled. I mean, ecstatic... you'd think I had found the treasure.

I continued my hike towards the edge of the ridge-top. Before I got to the final spot, I realized this was too difficult for Fenn to have made two trips. I retreated once again.

Here it is the middle of May. Despite being pretty positive by now that Fenn did not hide his treasure chest here, I couldn't get it out of my head. I had to get to this area to see it for myself... the area I named "the imaginary line", where the Santa Cruz River enters the inlet.

Plan D: A couple days ago Michelle bought a kayak. I suggested we take it to Santa Cruz Lake for its maiden voyage. I'd drop her off at the boat ramp, where she'd set off and paddle to the opposite shore at the far end of the lake. While she paddled, I'd drive around to the trailhead up by the Overlook Campground, and Molly and I would hike down to the stand of cottonwoods where she would meet us. She agreed.

That night I could barely sleep. I knew, or was at least pretty sure, that I was finally going to get to see the

"imaginary line", both shorelines beneath the La Caja Pueblo Ruins where the inlet meets the river.

It was a gorgeous May day with no wind... perfect for kayaking.

Plan D started off perfectly. Molly watched from the end of the pier as Michelle paddled away.

It was an eight mile drive from the boat ramp, around the winding road through Cundiyo, and back the dirt road to the Overlook Campground and Trailhead. In less than fifteen minutes, Molly and I were headed down the trail. The Sangre de Cristos stood out on the horizon to the east, still displaying pockets of snow on the Truchas Peaks.

As Molly and I made our way down the twisting trail, we could see Michelle off in the distance, waiting for us to meet at our destination beneath the stand of cottonwoods.

La Caja Ruins

My destination
the imaginary line

Michelle in kayak

Michelle in yellow kayak, approaching the shoreline.

Our plan was under way. Michelle was checking the depth of the water along the shoreline. I wanted to wade to the inlet, if possible.

I carefully made my way to the water's edge as Michelle continued around to the inlet. I removed the bottoms of my pant legs, and exchanged my hiking boots for old, worn-out sandals to wade through the water.

Molly and I waited patiently for Michelle to return and give us the news. Was the water shallow enough the entire way to the inlet to wade along the shoreline? I crossed my fingers as my excitement swelled.

Michelle returned with bad news. The shallow water soon gave way to really deep-looking water... no wading was possible after about ten yards. I told her to paddle to the inlet and river and asked her to take a lot of pictures, especially the shorelines and bluffs, etc, anything that could be construed as a blaze, or anything that looked like a "special place".

As she paddled away, I had a good idea. Molly and I would climb up the hillside and cross the ridges on top, and then find a ravine or run-off to get back down to the water's edge nearer the inlet/river. I was in such a hurry I didn't bother to put my hiking boots back on. I clutched them in my left hand as I looked for a path upwards.

At first this seemed doable but then the terrain became really steep with scree filling the run-offs that I was trying to climb up. The footing turned treacherous and my feet slid out from under me every few steps.

I was even using my hands on the ground as I crawled along and up. I smelled skunk and hoped it was the vegetation and not the animal. I had lost track of Molly and hoped that she didn't find the skunk, or any rattlesnakes, or anything else. I now was consumed with only my safety as I approached 40 feet up the bluff/hillside and across the first ridge.

Soon I could hear Michelle shouting to me from below. I couldn't see her but knew she had come back to where we had been. She told me to turn around and go back to the cottonwood stand immediately. She found Molly perched precariously on a crumbly-looking pinnacle 30 feet above her, with only rocks beneath, not even the water. If she fell there, it would be bad.

I wasn't sure of my retreat path, but decided to try to go down the same ravine of scree I had used to ascend. Almost immediately, my feet went out from under me and I started to slide downward on my knees and elbows. I grabbed a pine tree branch as I slid by but a large rock continued and banged my left ankle... it hurt. Thank goodness the branch was sturdy and stopped my rapid descent. I stood up, sort of, and assessed the damage. Abrasions, trace of blood, no broken bones. I turned around and purposely sat down. I would ride down this ravine of scree on my butt. Still holding my hiking boots in my left hand, I began the descent. I thought of Randy. Obsession and over-confidence are probably the worst two traits when we search for Fenn's treasure. I was ashamed to admit I exhibited both of those this day with my bad decision, even putting Molly at risk.

It wasn't long until I was at the shoreline, Molly found her way to us, and Michelle landed the kayak so we could come up with another plan. She said she had found a good "special place" that I needed to see. She gave me her life jacket and off I went in her kayak.

A possible "special place"

... approaching where the river enters the inlet. A rock bluff on one side and a shoreline of thick willows on the opposite side. Definitely not accessible on foot, in my opinion.

I did not exit the kayak and search for Fenn's treasure chest at the "special place". There was no way Forrest could have arrived there on foot, and I don't think he used a boat or kayak or canoe to hide the chest. I paddled away, content that at last I had seen the "imaginary line".

As Molly and I headed up the trail, I turned around to get one last picture of Santa Cruz Lake. I could see Michelle as a tiny dot in the center of the lake as she paddled towards the boat ramp. It was a bittersweet moment for me. I had made many trips to this area to search for Fenn's treasure since last October, and now it was over.

As Michelle and I drove home, we discussed the day's adventure. Despite the abrasions, bruises, and her accidentally rolling out of the kayak into the lake (near the cottonwood stand which was hilarious but unfortunately not captured on video), we all had a great day... no, we had an awesome day!

As I was explaining to her how I was done there and how I'd need to come up with a new search location, a brilliant thought flashed through my brain... what if Forrest ...?   5/13/2016

Post Script:

Later that summer I took a journalist to this area... to the bridge in Cundiyo at the confluence of the Rio Frijoles and Rio Medio, along the trail in La Caja Canyon, and up onto the mesa top where I wrongly looked for the La Caja Pueblo Ruins. During her interview with Forrest a few days later, she mentioned our "search" and my solutions to some of the clues in his poem. Here is a small piece of their interview:

Reporter: Cynthia used that yesterday. She was asking me, you know, let's try to find the blaze, and here's what I think the blaze is, and she said look around, and we looked around. I didn't find anything that seemed out of place or different that struck me as being the blaze.

Fenn: I'm going to have to talk to Cynthia because... Why would you if you have clues to a solution, why would you start in the middle instead at the first one?

Reporter: Well she took us through the whole process. She took us to look where the warm waters halt. That's where she thinks the first clue is.

Fenn: Where was it?

Reporter: It was at the confluence of the Medio and Frijoles rivers or creeks into the Santa Cruz River. There's a bridge right there where she thinks the warm waters halt because they are shallow rivers.

Fenn: Did you ask her to show you the warm water?

Reporter: No I didn't touch the water.

Fenn: See there, she wanted to find the blaze so she manufactured a place where the warm waters halt. There's no warm water under that bridge, I promise you. But she backed it in. You see how that works. I could take you out in my yard and show you 50 blazes. But it's not going to help you find the treasure because you don't know where warm water halts. You cannot back it in. It doesn't work like that.

Reporter: So, in other words, if you don't start right, you're not ever going to get there? But what if you think that you've found where the warm waters halt?

Fenn: Therein lies the puzzle! And I rest my case again. **Find where warm water halts and let that take you to the puzzle because I can show you millions of blazes.**

Some searchers believe this is Forrest Fenn's secret treasure map. If they turn it upside down, they see words and abstract pictures within the drawing. However, when I first asked Forrest if he drew this map, he rolled his eyes and said "I wish I could draw that good." But he did not say a definitive NO.

the Page 99 Treasure Map

So at Fennboree 2016 my friend Frank asked Forrest if he drew this map. Forrest told him an old war correspondent who he has since lost touch with drew the map.

BUT, could Forrest have added to it for the book? I believe he did... and the words he added say FLY TAOS. The JF initials stand for Just Forrest and there's a propeller above the JF.

I believe there's a propeller in front of the FLY TAOS above the red arrow in the picture below.

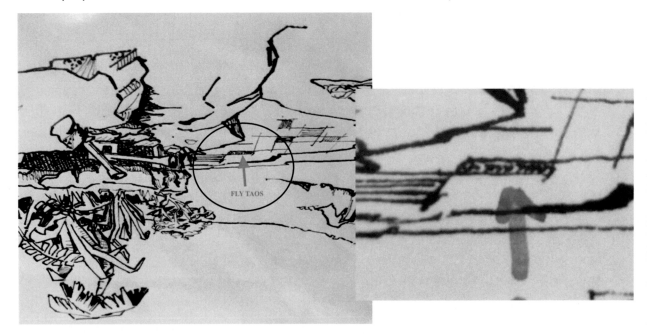

FLY TAOS

Forrest Fenn's Scrapbooks

These stories written by Forrest over the last 6 years are posted on Dal Neitzel's blog The Thrill of the Chase. Many searchers believe Forrest puts cryptic "hints" in these scrapbooks.

Here is an example, one of the "Rabbit Holes" I fell for: Scrapbook One Hundred Seven posted November 2014. Look at the bent corner on the $5 dollar bill. The word "treasure" is hidden beneath it. On my wall map, I drew a triangle using 3 peaks named for what I thought could be hints from the Tea with Olga story in TTOTC. **Red** Dome to **Black** Mountain to **Green** Mountain, and then a final line from Touch Me Not Mountain to make a right triangle.

I placed a cut-out of that bent corner into the triangle and looked at the spot where the word treasure lay.
Holy smokes, could this be a cryptic clue to the location of Fenn's treasure chest! (I also noted the mirror image of that same line.)

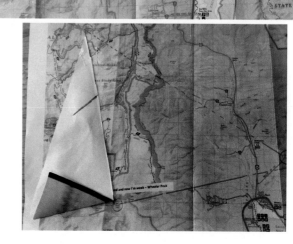

113

Clue NINE

But baby scant with marvel gaze

Just take the chest

Winter was excruciatingly long this year (2017), or at least in the Sangre de Cristos north of Santa Fe. I spent the winter months studying Fenn's poem, rereading, and rereading again, The Thrill of the Chase, looking at every sentence, analyzing every word, to uncover the hints he says are there... the hints that might be useful in solving the clues in the poem. I examined my wall maps, perused Goggle Earth, studied Forrest's scrapbooks, and stayed away from searchers' comments on the blogs. It was depressing. I felt no closer to the treasure chest than I'd been in the past four years.

Then in February, I made a paper copy of the bent corner (forming a triangle) of the $5 bill in Scrapbook 107 where the word "treasure" lies beneath. I overlaid it with the triangle on my giant wall map marking Red Dome, Black Mountain, Green Mountain, and a final line from Touch-Me-Not-Mountain west to Red Dome, forming a perfect right triangle. The word "treasure" crossed the end of FR58, close to where the bridge crosses the Middle Fork of the Red River and where the locked gate to Boston Acres stands.

February came and went. In early March I was hired by a Japanese TV production company to guide a crew into the mountains north of Santa Fe to search for Fenn's treasure. They wanted a real treasure hunt... one that met the criteria with possible solutions to Fenn's poem. There was still too much snow in the mountains above Taos, so I took them along the lower section of the Red River near Questa, followed by a day in the Jemez Mountains around Battleship Rock. I had searched both places extensively in previous years, and was sick of those areas, but had no choice. I kept thinking about my overlaid triangles... secretly thinking to myself that's where the treasure trove lies.

Mid-March arrived and I was sure I'd soon be able to search my new area. Molly and I made the 3.5 hour drive to Red River to check the snow depth. Holy cow... the snow in town was melting but the snow was still so deep at the end of the pavement off Hwy 578 I almost cried. I knew it would be at least two more weeks.

And then more storms crossed northern New Mexico in April... one after another. In fact there was so much new snow in Taos and Red River that the ski resorts extended their seasons. I was devastated. Did Forrest have a pact with Mother Nature to keep me from his trove?

I continued to do a few media projects in April... mostly interviews from home or an occasional drive to Taos or Red River but not to my secret location. This helped pass the time and allowed me a couple times to check the snow depth. I was chomping at the bit to get boots-on-the-ground.

And then I couldn't stand it any longer. It was April 22nd, three weeks into the month. We woke to a glorious New Mexico morning... blue sky and no wind. Molly and I jumped into the truck and off we went. I was ecstatic... my mind raced as I headed north. The poem looped through my head. I matched phrases from stories in the book to lines in the poem. I matched place names Forrest used in his latest scrapbooks to place names nearby in the interior of the Enchanted Circle. I matched geographic locations on my wall map to clues in the poem. But despite my excitement, I also allowed reality to drift through my mind... not that the treasure chest isn't there, but that it would still be covered in two feet of snow and unfindable.

As I made the right turn in Questa onto Rt 38 to head east to Red River, I promised Molly I would not stop and take more pictures of the mountain sheep if they were grazing along the roadside ahead. I already have 200 pictures of them, taken from the previous trips to check the snow-depth. Well, I broke my promise because I cannot help myself when it comes to watching the wildlife. But I shortened my gazing... and off we went to find Fenn's treasure.

It was no surprise that the forest road was still blocked with snow. I was prepared to walk the mile from the mud parking lot back along the West Fork of the river to Middle Fork Trail.

In all the times over the last 20 years I went back this road to hike, I had never walked it. Seeing it at a slower pace was quite rewarding. We happened upon this fisherman... fly-fishing for brookies in his own front yard. I was envious!

Molly enjoyed her day off her leash... I enjoyed my day off mine.

Thank you, Forrest!

As we made our way to our destination, I observed the areas around me... both along the river and up the banks and hillsides on the far side. Forrest said people have been within 200 feet of the treasure. He also said there are no human trails in very close proximity so I think the chest is hidden at least 200 feet from the road. This canyon is wider than some, and fits that possibility.

It took us 45 minutes to walk the mile to our destination. The snow was deep there. I knew we wouldn't be able to find the home of Brown or the blaze, nor did I want to continue another half a mile to the spring-fed pond where the warm waters halt.

But Molly and I did go beyond the gate. We walked a bit along the West Fork and looked around. I tried to imagine this area 200 feet from the gate... 200 feet from the foot-bridge that crossed the stream there ... without snow.

Notice the symbol of the bicycle in the bottom left corner. Forrest once said "what is wrong with me just riding my bike out there and throwing it in the water high when I am through with it."

Are there any rock- outcroppings where Forrest could have stashed the chest in a nook or cranny? I I couldn't see what lay hidden beneath the snow...

Was I disappointed? Not at all! Am I planning a return trip? ABSOLUTELY!

Stay tuned for part two...

A few pages ago I mentioned "Rabbit Holes"... a phrase searchers use to describe what they think may have been a clue or cryptic hint from Forrest.... something not in his poem, but something that will either help them solve the clues in the poem or direct them to the treasure. I showed a few pictures of the Tea-with-Olga triangle I drew on my wall map. Here is my solve, using that Rabbit Hole...

Boston Acres / Middle Fork Trail Solve

A few years ago, Forrest said "Many are giving serious thought to the clues in my poem, but only a few are in tight focus with a word that is key." What if the word that is key is GO... all upper case... "look at the big picture." O represents the Enchanted Circle and the arm of the G represents a paved road or stream/river that dead ends in the interior of the E.C. There are two choices that fit: the road to Taos Ski Valley / Twining (ff's story about his ball of string), and Rt578 from Red River to FR58 and the homes in the Upper Red River Valley.

To narrow down the search area and solve for Fenn's poem, I used SB107 and the colors of tea from TTOTC's chapter Tea with Olga. (See pictures on prior page.)

I drew a line on the paper representing the bent 5 dollar bill, where the word "treasure" is hidden beneath. Previously, I used a triangular piece of paper to represent the bent corner of the 5 dollar bill that was not proportioned correctly to the Tea with Olga triangle. In that solve, I was focused on Goose Creek and trail, which I now believe is incorrect.

Many searchers believe a mirror image is needed to solve the location of the hidden treasure chest, and I concur this is a possibility not to be ruled out.

Here (below) is the same map with red lines indicating both words "treasure".

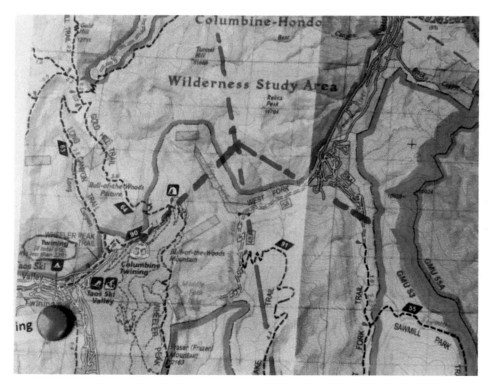

The red line on the right crosses the Forest Service road #58 to the parking area for Middle Fork Lake Trail and the Boston Acres area which is private property but runs along the West Fork of the Red River.

Two dotted red lines representing the word "treasure" beneath the bent corner of the $5 bill in Scrapbook 107. Both lines identify both the hidey spot and the road needed to get you there. The left dotted line (the mirror-image) crosses Boston Acres across where the word "West" is located (west fork). I believe the treasure chest is hidden between that red-dotted line and the symbol for the gate down the canyon from it. This is where the Mammoth Placer Mine is located, a potential hoB (home of Brown.)

The right red-dotted line crosses FR58 down the canyon from the gate into Boston Acres and the bridge across the Middle Fork of the Red River at Trailhead #91. This line indicates where you must park and put BOTG (boots-on-the-ground.) I have to walk to the spring-fed pond on the Boston Acres property (WWWH) and follow it down the canyon, not far, but too far to walk and find the home of Brown. That's where I will "put-in"... either from the Mammoth Placer Mine or possibly crossing the West Fork at the confluence of it and the Middle Fork. This should take me off the private property, maybe. I won't know until I put BOTG there.

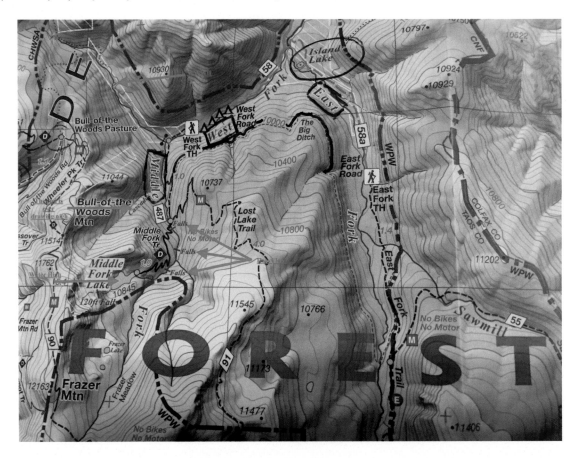

Forrest has been writing oodles of scrapbooks the last several weeks with possible hints to the location of his treasure chest. I sat up and took notice. Here are some of the hints identifying various place names within the interior of the Enchanted Circle:

3/03/2017 SB168 General Spicer ..."I suddenly felt like a crippled ant in an ELEPHANT parade." (Elephant Rock CG)

3/22/2017 Passages Two: Loom of the Desert by Idah MEACHAM Strobridge (my last name is Meachum)

3/28/2017 Passages Three: A Dark Date with Destiny The best book on the Custer fight, Son of the Morning Star, was written by Evan Connell, who was almost a hermit. (Star Lake)

3/30/2017 SB170 Wilson Hurley ...judge wore BLUE robe, my favorite color. (FF's favorite color is purple.) (Blue Lake) It was like a 40-pound turkey (Guajalote Park) staring at a June bug (JuneBug CG). He called the lawyers into chambers (Chambers Spring). I ducked that bullet with impressive form. (Waterbird Lake)

4/01/2017 Passages Four: The Price of Freedom It was an original wax model of a wolf. (Lobo Peak)

4/05/2017 SB172 The Sound of Bells ...their rings can be heard nine miles distant (Nine Mile Creek)

4/07/2017 SB173 The Prince of the Comancheros. Tied Jose Tafoya to a wagon wheel (Wheeler Peak, road, trail). Being a PIONEER is really fun. (Pioneer Lake,Creek,Trail)

4/08/2017 SB174 The Quahada Chief on a Black Pony (Black Mountain). His mother was CYNTHIA ANN Parker. my name is Cynthia Ann

4/10/2017 SB175 The Iron Rooster of Santa Fe County (Hematite Park))

4/11/2017 SB176 The White Fox ...but 350 big bills spread out (WILLIAMS Lake)

4/15/2017 SB179 Heck with Those Guys. William F Buckley (Williams Lake). Taos Indian models (Taos Pueblo, Taos Cone) Success sometimes hides in squinting wrappings, but a delicate new bow, if tied correctly, can widen eyes. TWINING

4/17/2017 SB180 The Unfortunate Hiccup-putt on the 10th green (GREEN Mountain)

4/18/2017 FF Vignette Butterfly Maiden – Kachinas = Kachina Peak

4/20/2017 FF Vignette Recycling Mistake – is this canister considered a relic? Relica Peak

4/21/2017 SB181 Doug Hyde in Full Flourish Picture of Al Simpson (Simpson Peak)

4/27/2017 SB183 Forest Gist and the Waning of Art (I hate that her birthday and Christmas are just 38 days apart.) Hwy 38

4/28/2017 MW Featured Question Walk Away...FF talks about school killings...is he hinting of "Columbine"? Columbine CG.

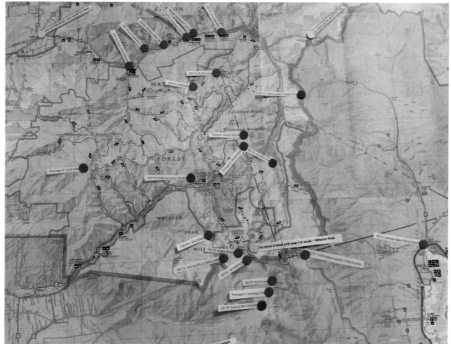

The thumb tacks and tags on this map represent the possible hints from these scrapbooks.

Part Two...

During the next three weeks, Molly and I made four more trips to the Boston Acres property and adjacent Carson National Forest at the confluence of the West and Middle Forks of the Red River.

We didn't find Fenn's treasure chest, but, oh, did we find a treasure! The spring-fed pond up the lane on Boston Acres is now "our special place".

The picture to the right shows the West Fork of the Red River above the pond.

These photos are from May 2, 2017.

Molly walking up the lane towards the pond...

... the mound is the Mammoth Placer Claim.

Molly and me sitting on top the Mammoth Placer Claim enjoying the scenery before searching for the treasure.   May 5, 2017

Soon after this search I received an email from Forrest mentioning what a beautiful place it is, and wondering where it is? Oh no, that means he's never been here... it was just another one of my "follies". I was guilty... I fell for some of the Rabbit Holes. Forrest has stated "Read the blogs for entertainment, and the poem like you were going to put an X on a map!"

Molly and I have been back since those trips to enjoy the scenery and share a picnic lunch along the edge of the pond.

Molly even went swimming...

June 30, 2017

Epilogue

After almost five years of searching for Fenn's treasure, I know 101 places where the chest isn't. For me, the quest to find the treasure chest was never about the money. It was always about solving the poem and matching wits with Forrest... It was always about discovering new roads, hiking new trails, and smelling the sunshine, as Forrest has so vividly put it. Along the way new friendships were forged... some of them will last a lifetime.

I still don't know for sure what the nine clues are. The ones in this book are in my opinion. No one will know they got them right until they find Fenn's treasure chest.

Forrest wrote, " So I wrote a poem containing nine clues that if followed precisely, will lead to the end of my rainbow and the treasure." I discovered that sometimes... the day's treasure is the rainbow.

Eagle Nest
Aug 25, 2017

I will never stop searching for Fenn's treasure until it is found, or my feet can no longer take me there.

Cynthia Meachum

August 1, 2017

Glossary

BOTG: Boots-on-the-ground

CCC: Civilian Conservation Corps

CNF: Carson National Forest

EC: Enchanted Circle

FF / ff: Forrest Fenn

GE: Google Earth

HOB / hoB: Home of Brown

HOD / hod: home of Dal (Dal Neitzel's blog)

HRTT: High Road to Taos

IMO: in my opinion

Jackie O: Jackie Kennedy Onassis

MW: Mysterious Writings (Jenny Kile's blog)

SB: Scrapbook (FF's stories posted on Dal's blog)

SF: Santa Fe

TTOTC: The Thrill of the Chase (Fenn's book)

WWWH / wwwh: where warm waters halt (the first clue in the poem)

YNP: Yellowstone National Park

Clue Number Picture Locations:

Clue One   Boston Acres
Clue Two   San Antonio Creek
Clue Three   West Fork of Red River at Middle Fork Trailhead
Clue Four   West Fork of Red River along FR58
Clue Five   Las Conchas Trail -- East Fork of the Jemez River
Clue Six   Lower Red River south of Fish Hatchery
Clue Seven Hamilton Mesa in Pecos Wilderness
Clue Eight   La Jara Canyon (these petroglyphs are NOT on this rock)
Clue Nine   La Jara Canyon (This is my REPLICA of Fenn's treasure chest. It is NOT the real one!)
Fenn treasure chest, TTOTC book, and Bullet photos used with permission from Forrest Fenn.

More FF Quotes -- The Importance of the first two clues

The most common mistake that I see searchers make is that they underestimate the importance of the first clue. If you don't have that one nailed down you might as well stay home and play Canasta. f

Fresh eyes and new thinking might provoke a winning idea. I would advise new searchers to look for the clues in my poem and try to marry them to a place on a map. (MW 6 Questions 2/04/2017)

"Read the clues in my poem over and over and study maps of the Rocky Mountains," he said via email. "Try to marry the two. The treasure is out there waiting for the person who can make all the lines cross in the right spot." (Business Insider 2/9/17)

Thanks, puttputt.
I know of a few searchers who have been reasonably close to the treasure puttputt, but there is no indication that they knew it. No one has given me the correct solve past the first two clues.f (MW Featured Question 4)

Mr Fenn, Is there and level of knowledge of US history that is required to properly interpret the clues in your poem SteveR.
No Steve R, The only requirement is that you figure out what the clues mean. But a comprehensive knowledge of geography might help. (MW Featured Questions)

You should start with the first clue and follow the others consecutively to the treasure. Hints in the book are not that organized.f

Searchers have routinely revealed where they think the treasure was hidden and walked me through the process that took them on that course. That's how I know a few have identified the first two clues. Although others were at the starting point I think their arrival was an aberration and they were oblivious to its connection with the poem. Playing a hunch is not worth much in the search and those who start out by looking for the blaze, are wasting their time.f (MW Question posted 6/25/2014)

Hi,
Did the same 9 clues exist when you were a kid and to your estimation will they still exist in 100 years and 1000 years?
Thanks ~Ron
Thanks Ron, thoughtful questions.
The clues did not exist when I was a kid but most of the places the clues refer to did. I think they might still exist in 100 years but the geography probably will change before we reach the next millennia. The Rocky mountains are still moving and associated physical changes will surely have an impact. If you are in the year 3,009 it will be more difficult for you to find the treasure.f (MW 6/25/2014)

"I would like to reiterate: Please go back to the poem and look at maps for your answers. Not every noun in TTOTC is a hint. If you can't solve the first clue you should not spend your money searching. My guess is that the person who is successful will very quietly solve the clues and walk to the treasure with a smile on their face." (Video at the Moby Dickens Book-signing)

I don't want to broaden the clues and hints I've written about by pointing them out. What surprises me a little is that nobody to my uncertain knowledge has analyzed one important possibility related to the winning solve. ff (MW Six questions yet again)

"I would advise new searchers to look for the clues in my poem and try to marry them to a place on a map." (Mysterious Writings Six Questions with Forrest Fenn Feb 4th, 2017)

More Fenn's Quotes about the Location / His Special Place

Expedition Unknown: Nov 2015
Josh: "Can you tell me why you chose the place you chose?"
Fenn: "It's a place that I have visited a few times. I have fond memories of that place."

"Get the Thrill of the Chase and read it; and then go back and read the poem, over and over and over again. And then go back and read the book again but slowly looking at every little abstract thing that might catch up in your brain, that might be a hint that will help you with the clues. Any part of some is better than no part of any. "

"Nobody is going to accidentally stumble on that treasure chest. They're going to have to figure out the clues and let the clues take them to that spot,f" http://abc13.com/news/millionaire-leaves-poetic-clues-for-treasure- hunters/685344/

I took it out and put it at a very secret, and a very dear place... private... and I walked back to my car, smiling.Telling myself, yeah, I really felt good. I had done something that I had dreamed about for a very long time.

I will say that I walked less than a few miles if that will help. I just looked "few" up and one definition is "scant". Why do I sound like I'm talking in circles. (MW 10/13/2014)

No specialized knowledge is required. My TTOTC book is enough to lead an average person to the treasure. (MW Questions with Forrest 6/27/2014)

What is wrong with me just riding my bike out there and throwing it in the water high when I am through with it? (HOD Forrest Gets Mail 10/03/2012)

Forrest, You said you made two trips from your car to hide the treasure. Besides walking, did you use any other methods of transportation to get back and forth between the car and the hide?
Thanks, Edgar.
Edgar, your wording of the question prompts me to pause and wonder if i can answer it candidly, yet correctly. Were all the evidence truly known, and I answered in the positive, you might say I was prevaricating, by some definitions of the word. And if I answered in the negative, you may claim that I was quibbling. So I will stay quiet on that subject. thanks for the question anyway. f. (MW Featured Question)

Curious about the long term fate of both the chest and the quest, I asked Fenn whether the clues in the poem will also withstand the test of time. "I am guessing the clues will stand for centuries. That was one of my basic premises, but the treasure chest will fall victim to geological phenomena just like everything else. Who can predict earthquakes, floods, mudslides, fires, tornadoes and other factors?" Fenn says. EARTH Magazine Feb 2015 On the Trail of Treasure in the Rocky Mts by Mary Caperton Morton

Your destination is small but it's location is huge. (MW Weekly Words 2/19/2016)

Snap Shots

pictures courtesy of Michelle Ummel and Tom Walker

Sipping from Jackie O's Korbel Brandy bottle

Jan 26, 2016

Cynthia sipping brandy picture courtesy of Sacha Johnston